Standing Ready

SWAIM-PAUP SPORTS SERIES

Sponsored by James C. '74 & Debra Parchman Swaim
and T. Edgar '74 & Nancy Paup

Standing READY

The Golden Era of Texas Aggie Football and the Beginning of the 12th Man Tradition

John A. Adams Jr. '73

Texas A&M University Press | College Station

First edition

This paper meets the requirements
of ANSI/NISO Z39.48-1992 (Permanence of Paper).
Binding materials have been chosen for durability.
Manufactured in the United States of America

Library of Congress Cataloging-in-Publication Data

Names: Adams, John A., Jr., 1951– author.
Title: Standing ready: the golden era of Texas Aggie football and the beginning of the 12th Man tradition / John A. Adams Jr. '73.
Other titles: Swaim-Paup sports series.
Description: First edition. | College Station: Texas A&M University Press, [2022] | Series: Swaim-Paup sports series | Includes bibliographical references and index.
Identifiers: LCCN 2021040342 (print) | LCCN 2021040343 (ebook) | ISBN 9781648430503 (cloth) | ISBN 9781648430510 (ebook)
Subjects: LCSH: Gill, Earl King, 1902–1976—Influence. | Agricultural and Mechanical College of Texas—Football—History—20th century. | Texas A & M University—Football—History—20th century. | Texas A & M Aggies (Football team)—History—20th century. | Texas A & M Aggies (Football team)—Biography.
Classification: LCC GV958.T44 A33 2022 (print) | LCC GV958.T44 (ebook) | DDC 796.332/6309764242—dc23
LC record available at https://lccn.loc.gov/2021040342
LC ebook record available at https://lccn.loc.gov/2021040343

In memory of Mary and Deck Autrey

Publication of this book is generously supported by Nancy and Leroy "Shafe" Shafer '67 and James C. '74 and Debra Parchman Swaim in memory of Dr. Joe Townsend '67—an educational visionary who touched the lives of thousands of students during his career as a high school agriculture science teacher, a college professor, a university administrator, and as a student advisor/mentor. Shafe and "Dr. Joe" were classmates at Texas A&M, and they were roommates while completing master's degrees at Iowa State University.

After ten years as a high school instructor at Guttenberg High School in Guttenberg, Iowa; Aubrey High School in Aubrey, Texas; and the Maquoketa Valley High School in Delhi, Iowa, Joe returned to Iowa State University to pursue a doctorate degree in education. Newly minted "Dr. Joe" was the head of the agriculture division at Illinois State University before returning to Aggieland where he served as coordinator of educational programs and associate professor of leadership development in the Agriculture Education Department, associate dean for student affairs in the College of Agriculture and Life Sciences, and as the campus-wide director of student development.

Throughout his career, Joe received numerous awards for his work as an educator, including the University Distinguished Teaching Award, Honor Professor by the Minorities in Agriculture and the Natural Resources and Related Sciences Council, and the Texas A&M John Koldus Student Services Award. In 2017 he received the College of Agriculture and Life Sciences Outstanding Alumni Award.

Dr. Joe and his wife Christine (Dr. Chris) served many years as academic advisors to Texas A&M Athletics. They were selected to the Texas A&M Letterman's Association Hall of Honor in 2011.

The lives of students and their families in Iowa, Illinois, and Texas are much better because Joe Townsend came their way. Texas A&M University and the College of Agriculture and Life Sciences are much better places today because Joe Townsend came their way. The agriculture industry has benefitted greatly from his advice and the outstanding leaders he sent their way. The world is a much better place because Dr. Joe was here.

Contents

Acknowledgments

Unbeknownst to me at the time, this project began in 1975 on a road trip with Richard "Buck" Weirus '42, executive director of the Association of Former Students. We were going to Dallas to visit with a number of Aggies. Our final stop of the day was at Turtle Creek to visit with Joe Utay '08. Joe's residence was filled with sports memorabilia dating back over six decades. Shortly after, I returned to interview Joe, and the conversation and correspondence that followed was priceless. He was at the crossroads during most of the key moments in the growth and development of the athletic programs at Texas A&M as well as being one of the primary promoters of college football across the Southwest. The small, "ruff-tough" captain of the 1907 Aggie football team, Joe discussed his love of football and the background to the events surrounding the Dixie Classic game at Fair Park. His key role in this historic game was noted in the official 1922 game day program: "Mr. Utay is the moving spirit in this great contest, because he is probably the best qualified football expert in the South."

In the weeks and months to follow I interviewed James V. "Pinky" Wilson '20, Everett E. McQuillen '20, A. J. "Niley" Smith '08, and Asa Hunt '22, in addition to having a number of conversations with Dr. E. King Gill '24. All this was in preparation for my first book, *We Are the Aggies* (1979). In the late 1970s I had a chance to talk with L. S. "Tiny" Keen, '22, who played in the Dixie Classic, but we failed to go into detail about the game. One key person I was not able to interview for this project was Coach Dana X. Bible. The dozens of questions I failed to ask these gentlemen would fill volumes. First on the list of missed opportunities, I would have loved to asked the coach about the "wave" to E. King Gill, beckoning him to come down from the press box at half time of the Dixie Classic. I would also have loved to ask Coach Bible how close he was to sending Gill into the game during the final moments of the 22–14 victory over Centre College.

Those missed opportunities notwithstanding, I feel fortunate to have had the opportunity to have known and been able to capture the observations and memories of these gentlemen. It was a privilege to learn more about their role in the rise of the Texas Aggie 12th Man tradition during what has commonly become known as the golden age of college football during the early 1920s.

This project was rekindled a number of years ago when Donald R. "Buck" Henderson '62 quizzed me about looking into the multifaceted story of the Dixie Classic and the 12th Man. He urged me to research and tell the full story of all the personalities and dynamics of the events that day in Dallas. I realized it was time to dust off my boxes of old documents.

Additionally, I must express great appreciation to a number of individuals for their timely assistance in digging out as many bits of information as possible in order to craft this story. I'm grateful for the tremendous patience of the staff of the Cushing Memorial Library and Archives and the Sterling Evans Library at Texas A&M. The fall of 2019 marked my fiftieth year of research in the Cushing Archives, dating back to the period in 1969 when the old campus records were maintained in a dark and musty basement, presided over by archivist Dr. Charles Schultz. My thanks go also to those who followed him, who humored me at every turn of my research efforts. In addition to archivist emeritus David Chapman '67, Leslie Winter, Anton duPlessis, and Robin Hutchison were very helpful. I am especially thankful to Bill Page '76 at the Sterling Evans Library, whose expertise has been invaluable and who has turned over more rocks and opened more dusty boxes of historical materials over the past four decades than I can ever hope to enumerate. Bill is a fountain of knowledge about the heritage of our mutual alma mater, and I am appreciative of his diligence.

At the Centre College Library Archives in Danville, Kentucky, I was fortunate to acquire the assistance of Beth Morgan in locating documents that covered the intriguing Kentucky side of Texas A&M's connection with the Prayin' Colonels, their players, and their coaches. Steve Ellis, at the Danville Public Library, was also helpful. The story of the small-college football powerhouses during the golden era of the early 1920s—places like Centre College, Washington and Jefferson College, and Suwanee College—has yet to be fully told.

Charlie Fiss, Vice President of Communications at the Goodyear Cotton Bowl Classic in Arlington, helped locate information on Joe Utay's early involvement with the history of the Cotton Bowl and his promotion of sports in Dallas. And I especially appreciate Dr. Robert W. Robertson, MD, author of *The Wonder Team* (2008), who provided timely insight into the legend and lore behind the great Centre College teams of the early 1920s.

I would also thank Jerry Cooper, longtime friend and designer of the cover of *We Are the Aggies*, for his expert insight and comments on the manuscript. Equal assistance and timely comments were provided by T. G. Webb, author of *Battle of the Brazos* (2018). Along the way, Thomas Autrey, Linda Bair, Alan Cannon, Robert Hicks, John Keck, Tom Murrah, Louis Newman, Sue Owen, Ted Paup, Malon Southerland, Jim Swain, Woody Thompson, Carl Walker, John White, and Bill Youngkin offered gracious assistance with background information.

Without the assistance of all the persons and institutions just mentioned and the tremendous encouragement from Sherry, I could not have completed this work. Any remaining errors or omissions are my own.

Standing Ready

INTRODUCTION

> *That the A. and M. College has one of the most splendid fields in the state for all out of doors sports is not to be disputed. The air is cool and invigorating, also the ground is a trifle soft but not so much so to prevent good work. We have some superb talent in that line of sport here at present. A few of the new boys have shown themselves to be first-class players in every respect. No degree of excellency [*sic*] can be attained in "interfering" "tackling" and sprinting with the ball, without constant practice. The "Cadets" will have a "happy" task in attaining victory.*
>
> —"Football," *The Battalion,* December 1893

This story has its beginning in what is often thought of as the golden age of college sports that emerged in the wake of World War I. That period produced what was viewed at the time as a tremendous array of sports talent, media hype, a flood of money for sports programs, and a national identity molded by athletic competition and rivalries. Sports stars emerged from every corner of the country to capture the imagination of the fans. Bobby Jones in golf; Babe Ruth, the "Sultan of Swat," in baseball; and Jack Dempsey in the boxing ring all became superstars in the American imagination during this period. At the same time, college football stars emerged, including a boy from the small town of Prairie Hill, Texas, named Alvin "Bo" McMillin; a native of Voss, Norway, by the name of Knute Rockne; Illinois farmhand Red Grange; a skinny 130-pound kid from East Texas known as Sam Houston Sanders; and a tall, lanky city athlete from Dallas by the name of E. King Gill. All had speed, a tough style of running, a wide competitive streak, and star-quality appeal.[1]

Along with the players, a new breed of highly competitive coaches arose to recruit, train, and manage this new talent. This was the era of men like Amos Alonzo Stagg, George "the Gipper" Gipp, and Glenn "Pop" Warner. In the South, Charlie B. Moran and Dana X. Bible acquired reputations as mentors of championship squads. By 1920, college football had become big business, commanding larger stadiums, coaches' salaries exceeding the pay of university presidents, and a struggle to define and establish the divide between amateur and professional status. It was in this environment that Texas A&M also basked in the success of its football teams, leading to one of the greatest games in the early annals of college football: the 1922 Dixie Classic.

The mark of a widely recognized and ingrained tradition is the measure of how it stands the test of time and its broad acceptance. The 1918–22 era was a formative period for a new generation of esprit de corps at Texas A&M, adding lore and traditions that continue to this day. During this period, cadets routinely became known as "Aggies"; after a number of proposed fight songs, the "Aggie War Hymn" was penned by J. V. "Pinky" Wilson '21 and officially adopted; and maroon and white emerged as the sanctioned college colors. The Aggies even had a hand—via branding—in naming the University of Texas' longhorn mascot, when University of Texas students used a running iron to fashion the steer's name from the final score of their recent football loss to A&M. They transformed the Aggies' branded "13–0" into "Bevo."

In addition to acquiring a championship football program, the Aggies would participate in their first postseason bowl game, and this would give rise to one of the central tenets of A&M heritage, the "12th Man" football tradition. Indeed, few aspects of Aggie lore are more iconic than the 12th Man, which dictates that Aggies stand throughout each game to symbolize their spirit and willingness to step forward when called upon. Born a century ago, the genius of the tradition evolved from A&M's earliest football campaigns and its nationally recognized prowess on the gridiron, culminating with the dramatic victory in the January 1922 Dixie Classic, played in Dallas.

The Texas Aggies came gradually to football. Collegiate football first gained prominence among eastern colleges during the mid-1880s. Played initially as a club or intramural sport, football evolved into an intercollegiate game among primarily Ivy League institutions and their regional rivals. The game spread next to the Midwest and West Coast and then to the South and Southwest. Through the late 1880s, stories of the New England football teams gradually filled newspapers nationwide, yet there was very little coverage of football played in other regions of the country. College football programs in the South began in the early 1890s, and by 1900, more than three dozen colleges and universities in the region fielded teams.

Football was introduced at Texas A&M during the administration of President Lawrence Sullivan Ross in the early 1890s. Sul Ross, as he was known to all Texans, had taken the helm of the college and pledged to enhance its programs, esprit de corps, and contributions of the land-grant institution to Texas. Baseball, the first team sport on the A&M campus, was very popular, and cadet teams competed frequently against local city teams. Encouraged to allow football on campus, Ross agreed to the first games of football as a club sport in 1892–93, with Washington's Birthday, on February 22, 1893, celebrated by a campus game. The "Farmers" or "cadets," as they were known before the ascendance of the sobriquet "Aggies," played their first interschool football game in 1894. Enthusiastic coverage followed in the newspaper with the largest circulation in Texas at that time, the *Galveston Daily News,* reporting in late October 1894 under the headline "Football Mad: The Whole American Country Crazily Chasing the Oval Pigskin on the Gridiron."[2]

In 1920, college football was still in its infancy in many ways. Rules changed and were modified yearly and sometimes regionally, while the point system, as well as the shape of the field and the football—the "spheroid"—were often altered. The forward pass was just becoming a new scoring weapon. Still, America embraced the explosive growth of football, which quickly became second in popularity only to baseball. Much of the terminology of those early days still exists, yet much has changed. For example, blocking was called "interference," a term that has today a different meaning. Because the context of this presentation is the way in which the game was played and viewed during the early 1920s, this term and others of the era will be used. Times have changed, but the excitement created cannot be mistaken. Even with the advent of the professional sport, college football has clearly grown into a national pastime. Indeed, college football preceded the formal rise of professional teams and leagues, which trace their roots to the 1919–20 period, the heart of this golden era of college football.

The game dubbed the Dixie Classic, in addition to acting as the precursor to what we now know as the Cotton Bowl Classic, was an icon of the period and occasioned the inception of the Texas A&M 12th Man tradition, which would impact football and its many participants as an integral part of both collegiate football history and enduring Texas Aggie lore.

* * *

One interesting precursor to the 12th Man tradition may, strangely, be found in an incident at the December 1912 Texas A&M–Oklahoma football game, as reported in the *Houston Post:*

> Governor Oscar Colquitt was one of the most enthusiastic and concerned spectators at the gridiron game. Early in the first half, when the visitors from Oklahoma threatened to overwhelm the A. and M. team, the governor moved to the edge of his seat and shouted encouragement, the prospects of victory seemed bleak indeed.
>
> Finally when the tension became more than he could bear with equanimity the governor uprose in his seat. Facing the field on which the conflict of brain and brawn was raging he addressed the warriors of the A. and M. in a voice which carried clearly to the confronting goal posts.
>
> "Don't let them beat you, boys," he shouted. "Hold steady and fight for every yard. Remember you are upholding the football supremacy of this grand State and for all of us—we want to see you win. You will win—you must win!"
>
> Cheers from the partisans of A. and M. interrupted the governor, responding, "Go to it."
>
> "If you need my help, he exclaimed, "put me in as center or fullback, or whatever you need me, and I will help score a victory."
>
> The Aggie defense stiffened, the offense became more aggressive and by the middle of the second half A. and M. smothered Oklahoma under a score of 28–6.[3]

> Squads left! Squads right!
> Farmers, Farmers, we're all right.
> Load, ready, aim, fire—Boom!
> A&M! Give us room!

A final note must be added to this introduction. As this book will describe, Dana X. Bible, head coach of the A&M football team during the period of this study, made many positive and lasting contributions while at the college. But, as will be further clarified in the book, he was a flawed individual. Most notably, while here, he was a member of the Ku Klux Klan. Indeed, if certain traditions have basis in fact, during the 1920s, as with many insti-

Governor Oscar Colquitt (in white hat) observes a yell leader and yell practice with cadets during the fall of 1912. (Source: Longhorn, *1913)*

tutions across the American South, Texas A&M administrators, faculty, and staff were expected, or at the very least assumed, to be members of this racist, vigilante organization.

To date, research has uncovered few written records of the Klan's activities on the College Station campus during that time, though enrollment at the college was certainly limited to whites, and no persons of color were permitted on the faculty or professional staff. Without question, the Ku Klux Klan was a violent, terrorizing organization, and its tenets, both in the past and today, deserve nothing but repudiation. Bible's membership in it, while perhaps a function of his time and the social class of which he was a member, remains as one of many facts of American society during this era that are deeply to be regretted and never repeated.[4]

More positively, the enthusiastic school spirit surrounding the new era of college sports, which Bible was so instrumental in building at A&M, has grown over time to embrace much more than athletic endeavors, encompassing student service, mutual support, and dedication in all aspects of campus life.

CHAPTER 1

Farmers Fight

Oh! There was no blame, and there was no shame,
To sting the Colonels like brands red hot,
For the Colonels knew full well,
That the Aggies gave them Hell,
And the Colonels were clearly out fought.

—"A Team There Was,"
Longhorn, 1922

The excitement and mystique surrounding classic sporting events tend to become legend over time. The list of such iconic events—whether team or individual accomplishments—has long been subject to endless debate and rankings. Retelling stories of competitive victories and defeats has been a part of history since at least the time of Alexander the Great. Some performances, such as Jesse Owens's victories at the 1936 Olympics in Berlin, will be chronicled as outstanding achievements and legends as long as sports records are kept. Indeed, Owens was one of the first great sportsmen I met, back in 1969.

In the case of sports across America, numerous moments have captured not just the day-after headlines and buzz but also a place in sports history and legend. While the athletic programs at Texas A&M University have had many memorable performances, the thrust of this work is to highlight the events, personalities, and legends surrounding one of the most iconic moments in sports history, not just in Texas but also nationwide—the 1922 Dixie Classic in Dallas, Texas, contested between Texas A&M and Kentucky's Centre College.

In the case of Texas A&M, sports have provided a defining link among the students, former students (alumni), and fans, as well as with various traditions that have emerged to help form the image of the university. Traditions reflect the values and image of a university, as they do with any long-standing organization. In the more than a century of Texas A&M sports, and particularly football, there have been a number of pivotal games, yet four gridiron matches stand out as exceptionally memorable. In descending order:

- 1940: The January 1940 Sugar Bowl game in New Orleans against powerhouse Tulane. A&M's victory sealed the first and only consensus National Football Championship for the Fightin' Texas Aggies (for their 1939 season).
- 1968: The New Year's Day Cotton Bowl game against the Alabama Crimson Tide. In this dramatic win over 'Bama, the Aggies' coach, Gene Stallings, secured the victory over his mentor, the legendary Paul "Bear" Bryant. The picture of the Bear carrying Stallings off the field is one of the best-known images in football history.
- 1999: The Texas A&M–Texas game in College Station following the Aggie Bonfire collapse, a tragedy that took twelve Texas Aggie lives, was one of the most emotional and tragic events in the state's sporting history. While A&M was the underdog, the Aggie team went on to win the emotional game.
- January 2, 1922: The Dixie Classic in Dallas, with a victory over the national powerhouse and highly favored Centre College "Prayin' Colonels" of Danville, Kentucky. Much of the national sports media in the days and weeks after the game heralded the game as "the greatest game ever played," altering the national perception of southern sports.

Other games may be considered and debated for this short list of Texas A&M's most memorable sports events, such as the 1986 Cotton Bowl victory over Auburn and star Tiger running back and Heisman recipient Bo Jackson, or the Johnny Manziel–inspired victory over Alabama in Tuscaloosa in November 2012, where the Aggies defeated the number-one-ranked team in the nation, propelling the young quarterback toward becoming the first freshman to win the Heisman Trophy. The debate over which games and moments to include in future assessments and rankings will go on and on. Only time and memory will tell as these games and other milestones find their place in college sports lore.

Thus, a brief review of the early years of football at Texas A&M is needed to set the stage prior to describing the classic game at Fair Park in Dallas on the afternoon of January 2, 1922, and its lasting ramifications and impact.

HOWLING WOLVES

The A&M College of Texas opened its doors on October 4, 1876, to six students. Growth was steady, with 144 cadets enrolled by December. In terms of traditions and activities, the dominant feature of the nascent A&M College campus from its inception and throughout the decades has been the Corps of Cadets. The campus as well as its inhabitants were as raw and tough as the times and environment in which they lived. One former cadet, William A. Trenckmann '78 (1878), noted the campus was "in a still somewhat pioneer time, large herds of deer frequently ran across the drill field, and for a time a Mexican lion would prowl about our student home, seeking prey held at bay by the howling wolves [most likely coyotes] that serenaded during the moonless nights."[1]

Cadets lived in the upper rooms of Old Main and Gathright Hall. There was no running water, no central heating, no telephone service, and no electricity. Daily classes, lab work, assigned daily chores (from chopping wood to hauling water), routine inspections, and military drill dominated the six-day academic week. With a near-complete void of on-campus recreational activities or sports to ease boredom, some cadets resorted to gambling, an occasional keg of beer smuggled in from Bryan, and other idle-time pursuits that, while officially not tolerated, clearly offered a bit of diversion. Bare-knuckle fistfights between cadets generally settled disputes. The holidays of Thanksgiving, Christmas, and San Jacinto Day (April 21, when cadets would go to the Brazos River to swim and cool off) followed by week-long commencement exercises in June were the only deviation from the rigid daily routine. There were no sports teams and few extracurricular activities—at least, few approved activities.[2]

The direct and active role of former cadets—those who had "worn the gray," a reference to the cadets' uniforms—would emerge as a critical factor in the survival of the young college, providing a valuable early base of support. Former cadets' sense of obligation to their alma mater developed swiftly. The highly supportive response by former cadets—who typically understood that outside their collective efforts, few others had a stake in the new college—proved pivotal in the formative years. The base for the Ex-Cadets Association, forerunner of the Association of Former Students, was established as a legacy of very active and dedicated alumni that continues to this current day. The support of and encouragement to expand campus athletics would soon provide a strong link between current and former students.[3]

THE 1880S

The decade of the 1880s proved a defining period of adjustment for the young college, its faculty and staff, and the rambunctious cadets. New president John G. James, an 1866 Virginia Military Institute graduate, was selected to replace Thomas Gathright. He quickly restructured the curriculum to a three-year program, hired new faculty, and worked to improve conditions on campus, including a dependable water supply. On Christmas Eve 1882, headlines in the *Galveston Daily News* hailed the completion of the first operational telephone line to the campus from Bryan, five miles north. During the 1880s, faculty became more involved in providing and promoting activities on campus. A number of literary clubs were formed, yet these tended to be exclusive and secretive. In response to this void, the balance of the cadets, acting on their own, formed mostly unauthorized, underground clubs such as the SOLs (Stay Out Late), the TTs (True Texans), the Fat Man's Club, and the Red Head Club, which was quick to coin its own "yell" long before the support of sports teams, a marching band, and yell leaders:

> Red, red, red, are we.
> The reded [*sic*] headed men
> Of the AMC![4]

Sports, except for an occasional pickup baseball game and some lawn tennis, were still not a part of life on campus. The cadets passed much of their free time scheming the best means to avoid chores, drill, and the mandatory inspections, hiking to Bryan for an evening out, or shooting wild game to barbecue. The campus YMCA encouraged recreational events, regularly sponsoring track-and-field days. The most exciting prospect for many cadets was to obtain a free round-trip rail pass on the Houston and Texas Central Railway (H&TC) for a visit to Houston.[5]

Successive regular US Army officer commandants and their small staffs assigned to the college were tasked by the administration with enforcing discipline from 6:00 a.m. reveille to lights-out at taps by 10:00 p.m. among teenagers who had no such formal training or regimentation prior to arriving. The commandant endeavored to improve the uniforms, increase drill, and occupy idle time with rifle drill and target practice events, which were very popular with the cadets. A military honor guard, the Scott Guards, later named the Ross Volunteers, was formed in 1888 and is considered the oldest continuously active student organization in the State of Texas. Efforts to organize musical groups occurred in late 1889 and early 1890 with the appearance of the College String Band. And the first Texas A&M class ring was designed by the Class of '89 (1889), featuring four very small diamonds set on a gold crest of an intertwined "AMC."[6]

Still, the A&M College by the late 1880s was in much the same condition as it had been at the start of the decade. The stalled growth (in spite of the fact that tuition, originally set at $197, was dropped from $100 a semester to $65) resulted in faculty turnover and sluggish access to much-needed funding. A hostile news media constantly questioned the role and worth of the fledgling college. Agricultural organizations statewide demanded more practical instruction in farming and ranching and fewer Greek and Latin courses. Furthermore, the new University of Texas, which opened seven years after A&M, now vied with the A&M College for funding, with supporters of the university speculating on land and demanding more money for the Austin campus. It was time for new vision and a champion of higher education to lead A&M.[7]

CALLED TO THE COLLEGE

By the late 1880s, there was real concern both among the legislature and among opponents of Texas A&M about the ability of the college to grow and sustain the faculty and student body. Governor Lawrence Sullivan Ross had worked closely with the A&M board of directors to enhance funding for new buildings, provide an improved water supply, and secure farm equipment. Following the exodus of the chairman of the A&M faculty and with Ross in the last weeks of his administration in Austin, he was offered the presidency of the A&M College. Or, as the news media reported, he was "Called to the College" in July 1890 at a salary of $3,500 per year, effective February 1, 1891. The A&M College of Texas had found the new leadership and vision they were looking for.[8]

General Ross was truly a living Texas legend and brought immense prestige and public esteem with him to the office of president. Having grown up on the frontier among Comanches, he was known as a frontier Indian fighter, a captain in the Texas Rangers, and a heralded general officer in the "late unpleasantness." Following the Civil War, he had returned home to Waco to farm and ranch and to serve in a number of civic positions prior to being elected governor in 1886 by the largest vote margin to that time. For A&M, he was the right man at the right time. Detractors in the statewide media described the A&M College as nothing more than a school of "elaborate military peacockery." But with his reputation on the line, Ross reshaped the college's image and the public's perception of the true worth and contribution of the lone land grant college in the state. He raised admission standards, enhanced the agricultural extension outreach in each county in 1887–88, and secured more funding from the legislature to improve housing and dining facilities and to build a new assembly hall.[9]

The resulting stability during the 1890s under the Ross administration clearly marks a period in which the foundation for Texas Aggie traditions was created. In a matter of a few years the once-bleak campus took on an entirely new tone with the addition of new activities, organizations, and intercollegiate sports. In essence, Sul Ross provided both the prestige and the positive atmosphere that allowed the cadets, faculty, and highly supportive former students to craft an identity for their beloved alma mater.[10]

The dynamics of the change greatly impacted the Corps of Cadets and the image of the college. In the fall of 1893, a fledgling drum and bugle corps was transformed into a nine-member band and, with the help of local merchant, bootmaker, and musician Joseph Holick, became the Fightin' Texas Aggie Band.[11] Future cadet participation in music was encouraged with the formation of a small orchestra and the Glee Club, sponsored by Ross's eldest daughter, Florine, and known today as the Singing Cadets. New clubs, sponsored by Mrs. Morris, the commandant's wife, were authorized. The class agent concept was adopted; the *College Journal* was replaced by a monthly edition of the *Battalion* newspaper in late 1893; the first college annual, the *Olio,* was published in 1895; and the Ross Volunteers honor guard was expanded. Baseball and track-and-field programs were started, though they were primarily intramural sports. The *Battalion* would capture on its page-one masthead the essence of the impact of the Sul Ross years and his role and contribution in laying the foundation for generations of Texas Aggies:

> Lawrence Sullivan Ross, Founder of Aggie Traditions
> Soldier, Statesman, Knightly Gentleman[12]

GRIDIRON

But the two activities that produced the most interest and excitement among both cadets and former cadets during the Ross tenure in the mid-1890s were, first, the numerous out-of-town Cadet Corps trips to Houston, San Antonio, Dallas, and the San Jacinto Battlefield on April 21 and, second, the advent of a new game: football.

General Ross was well aware that the Corps was the best means to promote both growth of enrollment at the college and the school's image. Prior to the formal introduction of intercollegiate football, the Corps trips primarily consisted of attending fairs, such as the state fair in Dallas and smaller carnivals. The events were arranged by former students who secured special chartered train rates. The Corps would leave early in the morning and arrive in each city by noon to lead a parade down a main street, followed by a grand picnic sponsored by the host community. Cadets, family, and friends were then able to shop and attend the local fair or festival before boarding a late-night return train to College Station. Texas A&M was on solid footing under Ross, with the alumni editor in the special Christmas issue of the *Battalion* noting: "No doubt all ye old graduates will be glad to know of the excellent moral tone that pervades the corps at the present time. Discipline has never been better." Enhanced morale and a sense of esprit de corps would be a pivotal component in fostering the core traditions at Texas A&M, including those around athletics.[13]

News of football arrived in Texas in the late 1880s from reports of the "eastern" teams being formed, first as club sports and then as organized collegiate teams at Harvard, Yale, Rutgers, and Princeton.[14] Word of the game and the enthusiasm around it sparked the first appearances of special-interest articles in major Texas newspapers in Galveston, Dallas, Austin, and Houston. The *Houston Post* published a special section on the basics of football to "introduce the tactics and methods of the big northern teams." According to a feature published in the *Fort Worth Star-Telegram,* football first appeared at Texas A&M in early 1891:

> Robert G. Littlejohn ['92] bought the first football ever used at the A. & M. College. That was in [spring] 1891, when the present city assessor and collector was a cadet. Since buying the pigskin and coaching the boys in the rudiments of the great college game that year, Bob has not seen them play, although they have won several southwestern championships.
>
> But on the sidelines in Dallas this afternoon [November 1909] Bob is probably the most interested spectator at the A. & M.–Oklahoma battle. He is probably too interested to cheer for the Farmers but in all the excitement of the game his thoughts will hark to the day when he appeared on campus at the state college, bearing the strange object termed a football. [Texas A&M won that day by a score of 14–8.]

The first A&M College of Texas football team, organized in the fall of 1894. (Source: Cushing Memorial Library and Archives)

"In 1891, Major William L. Bringhurst [acting president from July 1890 until February 1891], General Sam Houston's son-in-law, called me into his office at the college," explained the city assessor and collector Wednesday before starting to Dallas to see the game, "and asked me if I knew what football was. I told him I did. 'Well,' said the head of the school, 'I have been reading in the papers about the northern and eastern colleges playing this new game. Why can't we start it here? It will be great exercise and great physical training for the boys.'"

So Bob bought a football, took it out on the campus, and told his fellow students that he would instruct them in the game. Bob was some pumpkins in those days as a baseball player, and had picked up knowledge of football around Fort Worth before going to A. & M. The cadets took to the rough-and-tumble game like ducks to water. In a short time they became the best players in the Southwest and, when the first football wore out, another was purchased.

"I want to see how different they play now from the way I taught them eighteen years ago," he explained.[15]

Notwithstanding the Bob Littlejohn story, the earliest record of football as a competitive sport at Texas A&M dates from the fall of 1892, yet as Texas A&M archivist emeritus David Chapman cautions, "The original newspaper accounts are clouded with misspellings and typographical error. . . . Add to this an unstructured game in its infancy, with players appearing and disappearing from squads at random, and you have fertile ground for confusion." The first Texas A&M cadet teams, from two or three cadet units in the Corps, were intramural in nature. The games followed a very loose set of rules and were generally played from November to February. Cadets loved the contact sport. By the fall of 1893, there was a more formal effort to recruit twenty-six cadets to organize a "permanent" team and a couple of practice squads. From those engaged in practice, the captains would field one traveling team of thirteen to fifteen select cadets "that shall answer challenges from foreign teams." The *Battalion* reported that the first A&M team would be named "the A. & M. F.B.T." Yet there is no record of actual, formal intercollegiate games in 1892 or 1893. The cadet campus newspaper had interesting observations in spite of the fact that few had ever witnessed a game: "We have some superb talent, a few of the new boys have shown themselves to be first-class players, yet no degree of excellency can be attained in 'interfering' [blocking], 'tackling' and sprinting the ball, but with proper constant practice should put up a stiff game." There was a lone game on the A&M campus to celebrate George Washington's birthday, February 22, 1893, with former student John Carson as organizer and coach, but few details exist.[16]

Rip-rah-ree! A. and M. C.
Hoopla-hoopla-zip-boom-
Rip-boom-rah-rah-ree!
A. and M. C.!

"Yell," *Battalion,* February 1894

By 1894, there were some ninety organized and active college football teams across the country. In the mid-1890s the playing field was set up on a grid 110 yards long, and a touchdown was worth four points, with a successful goal after touchdown (later called a free kick or extra point) adding two points. There was no forward passing allowed. The excitement on the A&M campus was captured in the January 1894 *Battalion:* "Football at the A&MC is surely the coming game, judging from indications of the present. Two years ago comparatively no interest was manifest in the 'Scrappy' game at all. Only last week was the game fully introduced into this college and has met with marked approval throughout, not to say that football has no faults." Attempts in February 1894 to schedule games with the Dallas YMCA team and an unnamed team from Galveston (most likely Ball High School) apparently failed to materialize, but the stage was set.[17]

The enthusiasm of the cadets and former students would be forever changed on the afternoon of October 20, 1894. A crowd of some eight hundred, many more curious about the new game than knowledgeable about the rules or purpose, packed Austin's Hyde Park to view the first intercollegiate football game in the state of Texas. The Cadets of A&M (a traveling squad numbering fifteen players) faced off against the "Varsity," or the University of Texas. The Aggies were outscored that day, 38–0, yet the game set in motion the emergence of an entirely new level of statewide interaction among its colleges: through collegiate sports. With no formal athletic conference in the early days, A&M coach F. D. Perkins and other college and club officials informally scheduled games for the balance of the 1890s. Eager to have a rematch, the *Galveston Daily News,* the leading paper of the era, reported an attempt to play a second game against Texas on Thanksgiving at A&M, but no game with Varsity materialized.[18]

Efforts were made to schedule games, and there are a number of indications that the team A&M fielded in late November 1894, captained by Arthur P. Watts '95, was a completely different squad from the one that appeared in the first game. The only mention of football in A&M's first published annual, the 1895 *Olio,* was a reference in the 1898 class history that "'fish' furnished some of the best material for the [1894] football team." The A&MC Farmers ended their first, short, semiofficial season on Thanksgiving Day 1894 with a record of 1–1 following a win by a "new reorganization of the team" over Galveston's Ball High School, 14–6. The first competitive Aggie touchdown was scored by Nicanor Valdez '97 of Hidalgo, Mexico.[19]

For the balance of the 1890s, there were no official college colors, no yells or yell leaders, no mascot, no marching band, and no fight songs. Yet during these years, football continued to grow with road trips to Houston, Dallas, and San Antonio. Not bound by any formal rules, A&M team coach H. W. Smith suited up to play tackle in a number of games, and "players" were routinely recruited from passing trains to play after at least one day of "class." Despite a dispute in 1899 at the A&M–Texas game, the Farmers agreed to play Varsity at the San Antonio Fair in late October 1900, and were outscored 5–0. In six seasons between 1894 and 1900 (there were no scheduled games in 1895) the Farmers were 14–9–2. Reflecting on the formative days of football at A&M, the 1911 college yearbook, *Longhorn,* noted: "Not very many years ago all contests [home games] took place on the drill-ground, the football equipment consisted of one pair of cleated shoes which the fullback wore, and there was no enclosed field."[20]

> Chick-gar-roo-gar-rem!
> Chick-gar-roo-gar-rem!
> Rough! Tough!
> Real! Stuff!
> Texas A&M!
>
> *A&M College—Yell Book*, 1904

HULLABALOO!

The first formal action to promote athletics at Texas A&M occurred in 1901 when the A&M board of directors hired George S. Whitney at a salary of $1,000 per year as "physical director" to "direct the athletic sports of every character among the students" and to take charge of the gymnasium and new natatorium. The director was also charged with developing an organized approach to contact sports that would help guide the cadets away from the traditional free-for-all campus brawls, known as "cane rush," which routinely pitted the classes against one another. After one such melee it was reported that "pieces of garments strew the ground, hair is occasionally pulled out by the root; many a brave boy loses a cubic inch or so of epidermis; but all this only tends to make them more desperate."[21]

However, when efforts were started to enhance the A&M college sports programs beyond a club-level activity and introduce a more formal schedule to play other Texas institutions in competitive sports, mainly football, a number of the faculty did not approve and opposed any formal intercollegiate play. Advocates of a broad sports program and irritated cadets supporting football soon involved the former students, who rallied with their unequivocal support of sports. The former students appealed to the board of directors, claiming that "athletics is conducive to the health and development of young manhood, resulting in the best interest of the college." In response, the board "encouraged" the objecting faculty to rescind its actions and support sports. The faculty gradually shifted its view when a joint committee headed by Henry P. Jordon '95 worked with the faculty in late fall 1902 to establish a student-faculty committee, the General Athletic Association, to supervise all campus sports programs. The committee's name was changed to the A&M Athletic Council in 1906. The 1902 Aggie team beat the varsity eleven of Texas, 11–0, to be crowned the Champions of the South.[22]

The balance of the first decade of the twentieth century was dedicated to improving campus sports facilities. Football was the dominant sport on campus by the turn of the century. To accommodate the growing campus football crowds, games were moved south of the main drill field to the old vegetable patch managed by professor of horticulture Edwin Jackson Kyle '99. Dean Kyle, as he would be known by all, was a near-legend for over six decades. He was the "senior captain" or cadet corps commander, president of both the senior class and the YMCA, as well as class valedictorian. A professor by 1905, he turned his attention to the development of A&M athletics. Improvements to the "patch," a 400-by-400-foot all-purpose athletic area, were begun in the spring of 1905, with the construction of a fence costing $378.07 followed by the purchase of lumber for wooden bleachers at a cost of $312.00. A covered grandstand, assembled with cadet labor, was added on the west side of the field in 1907, bringing the total seating to over seven hundred. The first official football game played on what would come to be known as Kyle Field was on October 7, 1905, with the Farmers defeating Houston YMCA, 29–0. Cadets in the fall of 1906 named the field for Dean Kyle, and while not official, the name stuck until the A&M board of directors made it official on April 28, 1956.[23]

Organized conference sports came to Texas with the establishment of the Southwestern Intercollegiate Athletic Association (SIAA) in March 1904. Texas A&M's first salaried coach was James Platt, 1902–5. The changes and improvements were well received by the cadets, staff, and former students, with the 1909 *Longhorn* boasting:

> Not many years ago our team was clothed in overalls and jumpers, and a tree stump was used for a blocking dummy, but now our football team is one of the best in the association, i.e. conference.[24]

CHAPTER 2

Moran and Bible

> *Charlie Moran was a catalyst in the chemistry of an oft-remarked tradition of closely knit fraternity of this military school; this brotherhood was a thing-in-being when he arrived, a more articulate thing when he left.*
>
> —Kern Tips

> *Coach Bible was a gentleman, a forceful leader, and a great moral character. He had courage to match the situation. He could take charge of all situations. He had the ability to organize a squad into a loyal and spirited group. He demanded discipline and respect. He was a man who could have been successful in any profession. I could still hear him say, "Captain, go out there and take charge; take command of the situation."*
>
> —Joel Hunt

The coaches at the center of attention of the 1922 Dixie Classic were two of the leading sports figures in the nation, even before the game in Dallas. Charles B. Moran, the coach of the Texas Aggies from 1909 to 1914, helped develop and energize the fledgling football programs at A&M in the years leading up to the arrival of Coach Dana X. Bible in 1916. At Dallas in January 1922, the two coaches would field two of the most famous teams of their long and outstanding careers. Both coaches, and consequently their teams, were known for fierce competitiveness. Moran expressed the basic philosophy both he and Bible held. Reportedly, a "sensitive, idealistic" faculty member at Texas A&M once asked Coach Moran how he was preparing his players for being good losers, and he responded, "I didn't come here to lose!" The head-to-head meeting of these two coaches would add to their reputations and that of their players.[1]

UNCLE CHARLIE

One of the most interesting sports personalities and, according to Caesar "Dutch" Hohn '12, one of his former players, "one of the most colorful figures in all sports history" during the post–World War I era of college football was Charles Barthell Moran. He was born in Tennessee on February 22, 1878, and like Bible, he began his football career at the age of eighteen. He first went to Carson-Newman College, departing after one year to attend Bethel College, where he was allowed to both play and coach the team. After graduation he became an assistant at Carlisle Indian Industrial School under the famed head coach Glenn "Pop" Warner.[2]

In 1900 and 1901 he was head coach at the University of Nashville. He left football in 1902 to play eight years of professional baseball in both the major and minor leagues. A majority of his time in the minors was spent in the Texas League, playing for Dallas, Waco, Galveston, Cleburne, and Corsicana. He was briefly called up to the majors twice, in 1903 and 1908, playing in a total of twenty-five games for the St. Louis Cardinals. Back in the minors, he managed the Dallas Giants in 1903–4 and played on that team until 1909.[3]

The Yell That Won

Rickety-roc-de-roc-de-roc,
Rickety-roc-de-roc-de-roc,
Hic! Hoc! Hullabaloo!
Zip! Zo-ree!
Texas! Texas! A. and M. C.

In 1909, Moran—"Uncle Charlie," as he was known to most—returned to coaching, hired by A&M Athletic Council chair Edwin J. Kyle on the recommendation of Joe Utay '08, taking the position of physical education director and assistant football coach on October 6, 1909. After the Aggie team won its first game at Austin College, 17–0, and then tied Texas Christian University (TCU) in a scoreless fight, "the A&M sports community" reportedly lost confidence in head football coach H. A. Merriam and he was, according to Kyle, gently "relieved." Uncle Charlie took over as head coach, winning the balance of the games and ending with a 7–0–1 record. This was the first undefeated season for A&M to that point. Moran's 1909 team beat Texas twice in the same season and again in 1910, when the team had a 8–1 record, losing only to Arkansas, 0–5. The 1911 Moran-coached team suffered its second defeat in three years, losing to Texas by a score of 0–6. And the 1912 Aggie campaign was equally successful, ending with an 8–1 record, recording a sole, narrow loss to Kansas State, 10–13. Uncle Charlie's teams in his first four seasons notched a 29–3–1 record, scoring 833 points to their opponents' 81 points.[4]

In 1909, after the second defeat of Texas by A&M in only a few weeks, the winning team that Uncle Charlie had promised to produce was the cause of a great deal of consternation in Austin among Varsity fans (before the team was known as the Longhorns). The rivalry was captured in this 1909 *Bryan Eagle* editorial:

> The game at Austin yesterday was the fiercest these old-time rivals have ever engaged in and both teams played with all the skill there was in them. There is the biggest bunch of disgust in Austin today that was ever huddled together at one time before in that old country town. That University crew are sore, they are raw, they feel like they have been skinned from their head to their heels and tabasco sauce vigorously rubbed in as a healing balm. They are kankering, gangrene has set in and the world to their eyes looks like a great big round green cheese. They hate the whole earth and all the inhabitants thereof. They are busted, disgusted and almost insulted. They have got that "gone" feeling; they are all in and feel like they would like to crawl way off somewhere and lay down and die hard.[5]

Coach Moran came to Texas A&M to win. He coached football, baseball, and track, all with no paid assistant. He worked hard and demanded a great deal from his players as well as expecting the unqualified support of the Corps of Cadets. He quickly grasped the essence of the A&M traditions, cadet culture, and esprit de corps among the cadets and former cadets. His down-to-earth attitude and rough but fair approach endeared him to the Corps and his players. When necessary, he stood up for the cadets against the faculty, and the cadets, in turn, backed him. He and his wife and young son, eight-year-old Tommy, lived at the Shirley Hotel on campus and were fully involved with day-to-day college activities. He gave his personal attention to improving Kyle Field, overseeing the addition of grandstands, personally driving a team of mules to "work" the playing field, and building a dressing room and shower. Moran was aided by the very popular Arthur "Blackie" Hunter, who volunteered to assist with equipment and player conditioning. The seating capacity of Kyle Field exceeded two thousand for the first time in fall 1911. Dutch Hohn recalled that Moran was very important in developing the well-known "Aggie Spirit," noting, "Moran wouldn't *order* you, he'd *show* you, leading the way. He came to football practice in full regalia [football uniform], himself ready to play. Many, many times I've seen him get disgusted with a player who couldn't carry out an assignment, and take the player's place. Looking across at the opposing players in the scrimmage, he'd say, 'Don't ease up on me. I don't intend to ease up on you.' He gave no quarter and he asked none."[6]

In former years, before the formal organization of an athletic conference for Texas colleges and universities, rules were lax and rarely modified even to address safe playing conditions. Given the rising number of injuries, haphazard local rules, and infrequent policing of recruiting, no one should have been surprised by President Teddy Roosevelt's threat to use his "bully pulpit"—to issue an executive order banning all intercollegiate football unless and until extensive steps and rules were implemented to make the game safer and reduce injuries. The result was the formation of the National Collegiate Athletic Association (NCAA) in March 1906.[7]

Moran, however, was concerned with player equipment; he increased protective padding and added helmet linings, even though players were not required to wear helmets. In an era before big budgets, equipment sponsorships, and sports endorsements, Moran was basically a one-man staff and equipment manager.

> Moran also fashioned a good deal of our football equipment. In those days players didn't have protection they have now; our only protection, other than pliable leather helmets, was shoulder pads made of leather, and like the helmets, they were pliable. Moran would reinforce both shoulder pads and helmets with papier mache, to make them tougher. Before any game threatened by rainclouds, Moran could always be found at the field house adding length to our spikes, to give us better footing on muddy ground. He'd take off the cleat, insert strips of leather between the cleat and the sole, and put the cleat back on. This extra equipment might not have been regulation, but it was Moran. He wanted the best possible for his teams, even if he had to provide it with his own hands.[8]

During these times, coaches sometimes recruited outside players, or "ringers," a couple of days before a game. The only unwritten requirement among teams was that these players had to attend one day of class to be considered an eligible player. The Farmers were not the only Texas team engaged in this so-called "recruiting" practice. The use of itinerant athletes who played with two or three colleges in a single season was a common practice among northern football teams. Pay for play was a routine practice, and the new NCAA's main task was to enforce a code of strict amateurism and a spirit of fair competition.[9]

Seabrook, 1910

Preparing the A&M team for the fall was Coach Moran's prime concern. Harkening back to his baseball experience, he recalled that teams prepared off-site for each season. With this model in mind and with the approval of Athletic Council chairman E. J. Kyle, Moran hired former Yale player and manager H. L. Andrews in July 1910 to set up a preseason football camp at Seabrook on Galveston Bay, a cooler location than the hot and dry College Station campus. Long before the legendary Paul "Bear" Bryant's "Junction Boys" football camp in the mid-1950s, an off-site Texas A&M preseason football camp was conducted yearly between 1910 and 1914. The first preseason camp started on September 1, 1910.[10]

Andrews and squad equipment manager W. Scott Moore worked with the Seabrook Hunting and Fishing Club to arrange rooms and dining facilities for the team and staff. Moran did not join the team training until after the first week, due to his professional pitching contract with the Dallas Giants in the final days of the league's pennant race. There was a formal schedule for the football players that began with early morning breakfast, prepared according to a strict training diet, followed by squad members and coaches reviewing the new football rules, penalties, and guidelines for the season before going to the field for practice.

After lunch was a brief rest period, where "generally most of the boys 'go to the hay' for a nap," then an afternoon "recitation hour" on the rules followed by two hours of drills and practice on the field. Following the required evening dinner, curfew was at nine-thirty. While the camp was closed to the public during the week, it was hardly top-secret, as reporters daily sent articles and updates statewide, with one writer noting that the team and coaches dedicated a lot of time to "rule-ology."[11]

The camp was a combination of hard-nosed training and recreation. Workouts were tough, as Moran expected the two dozen players to be in good physical shape and hardened after working all summer. Because Texas was primarily rural, most cadets grew up in farming and ranching families. And while some players might "come to camp soft and 'rubbery,'" they were reportedly "put to the rack before the training closes—no favoritism or preference—to get in an athletic condition."

Morning practice included a tackling dummy drill and a session on a series of correct ways to fall on the ball ("to regain the spheroid") when recovering fumbles. A great deal of time was devoted to "running signals" and plays, with emphasis on "end runs" and "forward passes." Each practice ended with a period spent on "interference," or blocking drills. One paper noted, "While customary for baseball players to train away from their homes, this is the first time in the United States that a football team has adopted such tactics. Coach Moran is the originator of the idea." The camp was reported to cost $600.[12]

All was not practice. After daily training, players were allowed to fish, swim, and boat. Reporters were somewhat amazed at the team's enthusiasm, noting that "every man wears a bathing suit under their football togs and as soon as practice is over, every one strips to their suits and goes on a run to the water." The team was hosted on a yacht tour of the bay and the players "tried their hands at seining," pulling in thirty pounds of fish (taken to the kitchen for supper) and a "three- foot man-eating shark"; most of the "land lubbers" had never seen a shark. On Sundays many former students, friends, and family from the campus and Houston visited Seabrook.[13]

In 1911, Dean Kyle selected Sylvan Beach at La Porte for the two-week training camp. In 1912 Joe Utay '08 joined the staff as "football manager and assistant coach," by contract, between September 16 and November 28 at a salary of $1,000, payable in full at the end of the season.[14]

The Aggie camp was moved to New Braunfels in early September 1912 and 1913, held at Frederick E. Giesecke's 86 Ranch on the Comal River. In 1914 the Aggie preseason football camp, expanded to thirty-six players, was relocated to Otto Sens's hunting lodge at Strang, Texas, on San Jacinto Bay. Each of the yearly camps ended the last week in September in order for players to return for the opening of classes on campus. Uncle Charlie's preseason camps were an innovation that proved very popular with the cadet corps and very effective for the esprit de corps of the team, as reflected in this assessment: "Bronzed and tanned by the outdoor work and hardened by systematic training they have undergone, the men are now in fine physical condition and very eager for the fray."[15]

Farmers Fight

The Texas Aggies had been toughened into a winning team. Moran's methodical approach to conditioning and practice shaped the Aggies into a well-organized and confident squad, as well as one with an abundance of esprit de corps. It was not an accident that the Aggies fielded a well-prepared and competitive team. However, the University of Texas complained to the newspapers and the administration at A&M that they did not like Moran because he played "dirty" football. The university abruptly decided in 1912 not to play Texas A&M in football as long as the brash Moran was coach.

Supporters, of course, countered that Coach Moran coached teams to play hard-nosed, tough, winning football. Hohn recalled, "All of us A. and M. men of course howled that Texas' refusal to play was a result of their getting beat so much." Another observer noted, "It had been obvious to almost everyone that A&M was getting under the thin skin of Varsity [UT]; otherwise, why would the big state university have refused to play the Aggies over minor issues?" A&M alumnus James M. "Cop" Forsyth '12 further observed that Texas blamed the break on a student brawl in Houston in 1909 and the implied threat that there would be more trouble in 1911. Remember, Moran's cadets had defeated the university's teams three times during his first two seasons: twice in 1909 (23–0 at Houston and 5–0 in Austin) and once in 1910 (14–9 at Houston).

With no overriding authority such as a conference to broker the dispute, rumors ran wild. Texas A&M soon was under pressure, because the biggest revenue-generating game was the annual A&M–Texas match, with gate receipts over $2,500 in 1909 and growing to over $8,000 by 1912. These revenues were seen as critical to support of the college's annual athletic programs. Professor Kyle had personally signed bank notes to pay off the annual indebtedness; such amounts of revenue were crucial for A&M athletics.

Depending on which version of events one follows, the A&M administration either refused to renew Coach Moran's contact or he resigned in early December 1914; perhaps both were true. The *Houston Post,* offering one of several reasons given for his departure, reported he was "retiring" to return to Horse Cave, Kentucky, to manage a "mercantile establishment." His final game at A&M was a victory on November 26, 1914, in Beaumont, where A&M defeated Mississippi, 14–7. After six seasons, Moran would depart with a 38–8–4 record—the best coaching record achieved at A&M for decades. With Moran's departure, the first of many winning eras had ended at A&M.[16]

It was a bittersweet ending. The 1912 *Longhorn* yearbook was dedicated to "our beloved coach" Moran. Concerned with their coach's departure, the cadets issued a special publication, the *Shrapnel,* to express their

The block Aggie "T" formed at halftime by the Corps of Cadets at Kyle Field in 1920. Note four yell leaders dressed in white. (Source: Cushing Memorial Library and Archives)

disappointment with his departure. The 875-member Corps of Cadets and the Aggie marching band, now eighty-one members strong, held a dress parade in a rainstorm to honor and bid farewell to Uncle Charlie.

The Corps, "under arms," provided an escort for Moran and his family to the train depot, followed by a yell practice led by yell leaders Victor M. Barracco '15 and W. K. "Runt" Hanson '16. Tyree Bell, team captain, presented a brief, impromptu tribute.

Within weeks of Moran's departure, the Southwest Intercollegiate Athletic Conference, known simply as the SWC, was formed, and A&M resumed playing Texas on Thanksgiving. But his leaving College Station would not mark Moran's last encounter with the A&M College of Texas.[17]

Moran's grit and winning attitude set the tone for Aggie football for decades to come. Eager to recognize their coach, the cadets crafted a song for Coach Moran, set to the tune of "You're a Grand Old Flag," that may have hastened the adoption of maroon, rather than red, as the official college color:

Coach Moran

He's a grand old man, though we don't like to brag,
And his worth he will prove to you soon;
He's the idol of the team we love,
That fights for the dear old *maroon,* Rah! Rah!

And we stand by him, though we lose or we win,
And our faith in him will stand,
Though others may be good,
Take your hat off to Coach Moran.[18]

In advance of the first visit by the Texas Longhorns to Kyle Field in 1915, games between the two archrivals had been played either in Austin or at a neutral site. Uncle Charlie sent a passionate letter to the remaining members of the Aggie team. The note read, "If you still love me and think anything of me, then BEAT TEXAS." The Aggies rallied to beat the heavily favored Longhorns, 13–0. This score would be a major part of A&M's rallying cry for years, including the branding of the University's mascot, a longhorn, with the score, which was quickly altered to "Bevo" in order to conceal the deed. And the "fightin' Texas A&M cadets" would go on to win twelve of thirteen meetings with Texas at Kyle Field over the next two decades.

The Rest of the Story

In retrospect, the cancellation of games between A&M and Texas in 1912 had a much more sinister backstory than representatives from the University of Texas merely disliking the way Coach Moran played football. A year before Moran's departure, talks had already begun to form the Southwestern Conference, with these talks orchestrated primarily by representatives from Texas A&M (Joe Utay '08 and Hal Moseley '00) and from the University of Texas (athletic director Theo Bellmont and Athletic Council chairman Dr. W. T. Mather) during 1914. Clearly there were a number of objectives: first, to create a league with a formal schedule; second, to provide an organization to streamline, codify, and enforce the rules; and third, to raise the level of public awareness of collegiate football in the Southwest.

Yet there was an issue that was even more concerning. College football was becoming very big business. Speculators and profit-minded promoters were keen to play a part in staging and promoting games in general and the annual A&M–Texas matchup in particular. To control as well as maximize their profits, sponsors encouraged the games between these two rivals to be played at neutral sites in Houston, Dallas, Beaumont, or San Antonio. The larger venues in these cities would ensure a larger paying crowd. Promoters justified this by saying it would reduce the "intensely bitter feeling between the students" that had resulted in off-field altercations during these games.

Meanwhile, the A&M football program continued to do very well in 1912–14 when it did not play Texas, forcing the realization that maybe A&M was not dependent on Texas for revenue. And the fact that the Aggies had a winning record of 6–1–1 in the fall of 1914 further highlighted the ongoing success at Texas A&M. An editorial in the *Austin Statesman* called for the games to resume and be played only on each campus, and for an athletic conference to be formed: "There are many good reasons why they should be played at home. We realize that money is essential too, for the support of a football team, but we believe that money is not every consideration in college athletics. The return trips [to campus] will show the old students the needs of their alma mater and will make them greater advocates of better things for their schools."[19]

The political dynamics between Texas A&M and the University of Texas have also been overlooked and underreported. As A&M grew and had an increased impact across the state with its academic programs, its extension services, and contributions of its former students in all walks of life and industry, the University of Texas and its supporters hoped to limit A&M's growth and legislative funding. The status of the state's Permanent School Fund was constantly in question. Texas A&M's success under Coach Moran only drew more attention to A&M from the citizens and taxpayers of Texas. Professor emeritus and author Dr. Henry C. Dethloff, in his 1975 *Centennial History of Texas A&M University, 1876–1976,* provides valuable insight into the political rivalry between supporters of the two universities:

> The Texas A&M–University of Texas football rivalry, which dates from essentially 1915, was in many respects a manifestation of the political rivalry which had existed between the schools even before the University of Texas had become a reality. Since the time of Lawrence Sullivan Ross, the political rivalry had been somewhat muted, or at least had been elevated to a higher level—to the board rooms and executive offices. As political rivalry cooled, athletic rivalry between Texas A&M and the University intensified and

seems to have been largely a by-product of modern football. But politics remained a part of the A&M-University "game."[20]

The fact that Texas was not on the schedule for a couple of years did not sway the cadets from the ongoing quest to land a fight song for the college team. Numerous songs were introduced, but none seemed to stick. One song that got consideration and recognition in the 1914 *Longhorn* but did not survive was "We Play Football" (to the tune of "In My Harem"), with a clear reference to the Varsity foe's unwillingness to play:

We Play Football
We play football, play football;
There is not a team in Texas
That can hold us for a minute.
Old Varsity isn't in it;
We can cheer our team, back our team;
We are there at any time.
All the college teams go down
When we come down the line;
We play football, play football;
We lead our team to victory,
Then the things we will do
Will make you wish that you
Were in our college at A. &.M.

D. X. Bible

Dana Xenophon Bible, best known simply as "D.X.," was born on October 8, 1891, in Jefferson City, Tennessee, son of Jonathan Squire and Cleopatra Bible. Dana's father was a professor of Greek and Latin—hence his son's middle name, from the famed Greek warrior of 400 B.C. Although he too was proficient in Latin, D.X.'s interests in sports and particularly football commanded his attention, thus precluding any career teaching the classics. D.X. attended Carson-Newman College and Brandon Prep School in Shelbyville, Tennessee, where he played and was first acquainted with coaching. In the early days of football the rules were flexible and eligibility standards lax, which allowed D.X. to both coach and play halfback on the team. The combination of his rugged looks and premature balding meant that he looked years older than his age, and he was often called "Grandpa" by players and rooters.[21]

Bible's first full-time coaching job was at Mississippi College, where his young and undersized team handed southern powerhouse Tulane a major defeat. In 1916, Coach Edwin H. "Jigger" Harlan recruited D.X. as the first Texas A&M freshman coach. With Bible, the first paid freshman coach in Texas collegiate football, Harlan's plans were to screen, develop, and better prepare the freshmen for the varsity squad. There was very little robust recruiting from Texas high schools, and most Aggie players were walk-ons, many of whom obtained their first taste of football playing in one of a dozen units in the Corps of Cadets intramural programs. Near the end of the season, the Louisiana A&M College Pelicans (their name before LSU was known as the Tigers) lost their head football coach with three games remaining in the 1916 season and approached Texas A&M about "borrowing" Bible to coach the last few varsity games on the schedule. Harlan and A. C. Love, chairman of the Aggies' athletic committee, agreed to the brief stay in Baton Rouge. Much to the surprise of many, in their last three games LSU beat Ole Miss and tied Rice and Tulane. LSU soon contacted Texas A&M about keeping Bible.[22]

"I felt a moral obligation to A&M," Bible recalled. "They had consented to let me go to help out LSU: now they wanted me back. I was delighted and honored to return to A&M as its head coach."[23]

Coach Bible had good reason to return to College Station. After only two seasons, and despite having a record of 12–5 that included a famous 13–0 victory over the University of Texas Longhorns at Kyle Field in 1915, Jigger Harlan was let go; according to Wilbur Evans, "the administration decided to replace him," and Harlan, an All-American back from Princeton, returned to his alma mater to coach the freshman team. The consensus recommendation to college president William B. Bizzell was to confirm Bible as the next Aggie head coach (the 1917 *Texas A&M Longhorn* yearbook pictured Bible with the title "Head Coach Elect") at an annual salary of $1,600. The 1916 freshman team Bible helped recruit and coach before going to LSU would provide the talent and leadership to man the first great Texas Aggie football team in the institution's long history. Bible was one of the greatest strategists in the game, and his approach involved an aggressive offense backed by a dominant defense.[24]

At the age of twenty-five, Bible returned from Baton Rouge to A&M to prepare for the fall of 1917 season. The members of his young freshman squad were now sophomores and eligible for the varsity. Standout players on the squad included Roswell Higginbotham, Jack Mahan, Scot Alexander, Tim Griesenbeck, and Kyle Elam. The season started with crushing wins over Austin College, 66–0, and the University of Dallas, 98–0, followed by a victory over his old team, LSU, 27–0, and a 35–0 win over Tulane, Bible's second win over the Green Wave from New Orleans. The heart of the 1917 season was the final three games with Rice, Baylor, and Texas—all A&M victories. The Aggies were crowned Southwest champions. The 1917 team, which went 8–0, was the first in Texas A&M history to go undefeated, untied, and unscored upon—racking up 270 points, while holding the opposition to zero. This was the beginning of the greatest five-season run of victories in college football history (33–3–3), culminating in the Dixie Classic victory over Centre College in early January 1922.[25]

Over There in the Air and on the Ground

The excitement over the fall 1917 championship soon died down as the country and Texas A&M prepared for war in Europe following the formal declaration of war against the Axis Powers in April 1917. Dr. Bizzell, the faculty, and the A&M Board of Directors in mid-1917 made a complete commitment of the cadets, staff, and faculty at A&M to supporting the war effort. Soon the campus became an extensive training location for critical areas such as aircraft operations and repair, radio operations, farrier training, and meteorology. Thousands of US Army and Navy inductees would be stationed on campus for training and then transferred to assignments in France, Italy, Belgium, and England.[26]

The resulting total disruption of the A&M academic programs required an overhaul of all class schedules as well as added housing and dining arrangements. The campus soon ran on a twenty-four-hour schedule at the direction of the US Army. To rush potential officer candidates to training, the Class of 1917 was ordered to depart the campus early and travel to Camp Funston in Leon Springs, Texas. Only weeks short of graduation, the members of the class were presented with their degrees and commissions at army training camp. By New Year's Day 1918 most of the A&M football and basketball teams had been inducted into the armed services, including Coach Bible. With the endorsement of Ike Ashburn, secretary to the A&M Board of Directors, Bible went to San Antonio, enlisted in the Army Air Service, and was immediately sent to training. The departure of Coach Bible, who also coached basketball and baseball, left a major void in the athletic department. The A&M Athletic Committee was very pleased with the tremendous success of the 1917 undefeated and undisputed champions of the Southwest. To confirm their appreciation, they voted to pay Bible's salary of $1,600 for the balance of the year and gave him "an unlimited leave of absence." Furthermore, prior to his departure, Coach Bible was informed that "when he returned to us after the war," his annual salary would be $2,400.[27]

Assistant coach D. V. "Tubby" Graves, assisted by athletic director W. L. Driver, took charge of the 1918 football team. In spite of the depleted ranks, the team compiled a 6–1 record, losing only to Texas in Austin. Enlistments continued to cut deep into the ranks of the Corps of Cadets, as all four team captains of major sports for the 1918–19 season were inducted into service: Eugene S. Wilson '19, captain of the 1918 football team, was assigned to coastal artillery training at Fort Monroe, Virginia; Edmund M. Longcope '20, captain of the basketball team, was sent to Fort Sheridan, for field artillery school; John D. McMurry '20, captain of the baseball team, was a lieutenant in the cavalry; and Jack F. Mahan '21, captain of the track team, was sent to coastal artillery training. Star A&M running back Roswell Higginbotham '21 left in midseason to enlist in the Army Air Service. As these cadets were starting their service branch training, Coach Bible was finishing flight school as a pursuit pilot and was in transit to France for additional training and orientation.[28]

Coach Bible received no preferential treatment, enlisting at Fort Sam Houston in San Antonio in the Enlisted Reserve Corps on December 15, 1917, as a private first class. He was immediately ordered to the cadet training program at the School of Military Aeronautics in Austin, and upon completion of the program, on March 15, 1918, was sent to ground school at Camp Dick. Soon afterward he was ordered to Taliaferro Field No. 3 in Fort Worth for pilot training. After completing this training in early July, he was commissioned a lieutenant in the Army Air Service. Due to his flying proficiency, he was made an instructor pilot. He was soon sent to Wilbur Wright Field in Dayton, Ohio, for advanced combat training and later to Mineola, New York, from which he was transferred to France in the summer of 1918.[29]

Once overseas, D.X. was assigned to the 22nd Aero Pursuit Squadron, known as the "Shooting Stars," of the First US Field Army at Soully, near Verdun. Following completion of the French School of Advanced Training at Issoudun, he was ready for duty as a scout pilot over the Western Front. Flight operations during the war were under the command of the US Army Signal Corps and were expected to be used primarily for observation flights and to help with targeting for the field artillery. Pursuit pilots, who were generally unarmed, flew at low levels to observe enemy troop and supply movements. In addition to flying routine pursuit patrols, Bible passed the time on the ground in France by coaching airmen in intersquad football and baseball games. With the pick of some of the top collegiate players on active duty in France, Bible was able to assemble an all-star team. The game of football was alive and well "over there," and the spirit of the gridiron was captured in this anonymous verse:

> But when the fighting Doughboy came,
> He brought his shifts and forward pass;
> And he can drop kick just the same,
> As when he played on Yankee grass.
> Shades of Spalding, Walter Camp,
> And others who our sports enhance;
> Who would have thought, two years ago,
> That we would have pigskin days in France?[30]

While the exodus of cadets from campus and the draft of trainees continued across America in the early fall of 1918, rumors among the troops on the Western Front were varied. All hoped for a quick end to the fighting, even as the American and French high command planned, re-equipped, and trained for a major ground offensive in early 1919. However, the uncertainty ended on November 11, 1918, when an agreement was reached to invoke an armistice and an end to hostilities. Bible and his A&M players on active service were discharged and returned to campus in the spring and summer of 1919. D.X. was pleased to welcome the old players and new cadet recruits and announced that the old "pep" and enthusiasm of the prewar A&M campus events and sports had returned. Bible's old friend and Western Front veteran Col. Ike Ashburn also returned to A&M as commandant of cadets and chairman of the A&M Athletic Council.[31]

BIBLE AND A&M IN THE POST–WORLD WAR I PERIOD

The College Station campus to which Bible returned in 1919 was, like the majority of institutions of higher education at that time throughout the American South and many in the North, racially segregated, in addition to being an all-male college with mandatory military training. Enrollment of African American students would not be permitted until 1963, the same year that the school's Board of Regents officially sanctioned the enrollment of women.[32]

As a white man raised in the South, Bible likely acquired many of the racial prejudices prevalent in his time and place. Though research has, to date, not uncovered any overtly racist rhetoric in any of Bible's public or private statements, his membership in the Ku Klux Klan is attested by the presence of Klan robes bearing Bible's name stitched into the collar, held in the Special Collections of Cushing Library at Texas A&M. The athletes he coached were all white, and the opponents' teams and coaching staffs were the same. Though this time is historically regarded as a golden era in college football because of the dominance of college and university teams in the popular consciousness—well before the emergence or wide acceptance of the professional sport—the game and its significance in this period must always be read against the background of the still-segregated society that nurtured it. During this period, neither Texas A&M nor Dana X. Bible, as head football coach, were any exception.[33]

Preparing for the 1919 Season

Eager to return to coaching and prepare for the upcoming season, Coach Bible was concerned that he had missed months of recruiting and thus encouraged all players that had left for military duty to return to Aggieland. This letter, sent to Richard "Chic" Harrison Jr., of Bryan, was also sent to Aggies statewide to encourage their return while outlining Bible's intentions:

> Agricultural and Mechanical College of Texas
> Athletics
> D. X. Bible, Football
> August 20th, 1919
>
> Dear "Chicken,"
> Guess you are beginning to show symptoms of the "Pig-skin Fever," if not, get around some of the "Old Farmers," catch a bad case and come back this Fall and get fifteen hundred others infected with it. Everyone is expected to put politics, business, and even their best girl aside and report September 15th, for duty at College Station. Blot out everything that will interfere with this arrangement.
>
> All men who left school to enter the services are eligible to participate in Athletics this Fall, also Freshmen will be permitted to play their first year.
>
> Many changes have been made at A. and M. which will, I am sure, make your stay with us more pleasant and profitable. Our outlook for a successful season is indeed encouraging. The old stars among the Alumni have promised to come back from time to time

and give us systematic help. A re-birth of college spirit has come into the hearts of every A. and M. Man, and I am convinced that the team that beats us will be champion of the Southwest.

If any information is desired I shall be glad to furnish it. Let me have a letter at once stating you will report on September 15th, ready to fight for victory, fair and square, hard but clean.

This is the motto for 1919: "They Shall Not Pass."

Cordially, Your Friend,
D. X. Bible[34]

"Rough, Tuff, Real Stuff"

The momentum and success the Aggies achieved prior to the Great War continued into the 1919 season. Due to the disruption of the war, all college athletes were given one extra year of eligibility to play. Returning players from the 1917 team and members from the 1918 squad quickly continued the string of victories. Behind a large line led by "Woodrow" Wilson, the first A&M lineman to be team captain, Mahan, Weir, and company beat Texas 7–0 at Kyle Field and completed the college's second undefeated, untied, and unscored-upon season, outscoring opponents 275–0. A&M was once again crowned champions of the Southwest. The statistics, viewed by today's standards, are incredible. The combined 1917 and 1919 seasons represent a record of 18 wins while outscoring opponents 545–0. Thus, the three-season record compiled in 1917, 1919, and 1920 by Dana X. Bible was an impressive 24 victories and 1 loss.[35]

Coach Bible and his team received wide recognition and press coverage across the Southwest, but not much attention outside the state of Texas. D. X. received no bonus, and up until 1921, the Aggies had participated in no postseason games. Bible, in addition to being head football coach, continued to coach the baseball and basketball teams. He once again began the freshman football program and scheduled a few games to evaluate his new cadet talent. During spring practice in April 1921, star running back Jack Mahan was selected team captain. Most of the star players from the past two years had graduated, and the Aggie ranks began with a dozen new players. Teams across Texas, Oklahoma, and Louisiana had also recruited heavily to rebuild their postwar programs. Bible welcomed the improved collegiate competition, because it raised the image of college football across the South and Southwest. However, the news media, even in stories printed in papers across Texas, concentrated much of the attention on the exploits of East Coast teams: Harvard, Yale, Princeton, and Rutgers.

Aggie team captain W. C. "Heine" Weir '23 and coach D. X. Bible in 1921. Weir was injured on the third play of the Dixie Classic and sidelined. (Source: Cushing Memorial Library and Archives)

However, an upstart team in Danville, Kentucky, basking in growing news media attention, would be the first wedge in shifting the attention on the national football landscape to the South and Southwest. That team was coached by none other than Charlie Moran.[36]

Rules were constantly being updated to include a schedule of penalties, often printed in the game-day program. With no public address system, the umpire would relay the infraction to the scorekeeper, who would, "whenever possible," post the number of the infraction listed on the scoreboard. The program generally listed about forty different numbered infractions and penalties, including the following examples:

1921 Football Infractions and Penalties

Number	Infraction	Penalty
1.	Attempted to draw opponents offside	5 yards
2.	Coaching from sidelines	15 yards
3.	Crawling	5 yards
4.	Delay in starting second half	25 yards
12.	Hurdling	15 yards
17.	Interference with fair catch	15 yards
19.	Kicking loose ball	Loss of ball
25.	Offside, both sides	No penalty
27.	Piling up (on)	15 yards
33.	Slugging	Half distance to goal and disqualification
38.	Tripping	15 yards
40.	Unsportsmanlike conduct	15 yards[37]

The tremendous support from former students for the Aggie football team resulted in an expansion of the wooden bleachers in Kyle Field, efforts to improve the playing surface, new uniforms and equipment, and an extensive interest and attendance by former students and fans of the Aggies, still often called the "Farmers" or "Cadets" in the media.

While there were banners and promotion of the school spirit often referring to the "crimson [maroon] and white," the football uniforms remained a mix of dull black and gray with a dark stripe through the midsection of the jersey. In the fall of 1921, numbers were sewn on the A&M players' jerseys for the first time, but only on the back.[38]

There was gradual improvement in player equipment as the NCAA became more concerned with severe injuries nationwide. Safety for the players gained more attention, and new equipment to reduce injuries was strongly encouraged. Players were now required to wear heavier padded leather helmets (no longer optional) during the entire game. The forward pass was allowed, and penalties increased for infractions. The new rules barred both freshmen and graduate students from participating in intercollegiate sports, and eligibility was limited to three years. Furthermore, all game officials would be independently assigned to each college game rather than selected by the coaches of either team. However, there were no clear recruiting standards and only lax monitoring or enforcement of academic eligibility.[39]

Coach Bible presented a clear focus on the role of the defense in his book *Championship Football*, noting, "A familiar football cliché is: A good offense is the best defense. There is some truth in it of course, but all of us have seen a team with a good offense take a bad licking—because its opponent had a good offense *and* a sturdy defense that enabled it to gain control of the ball. A great offense can keep the ball, but first it has to *get* the ball." Bible coached these key elements of a sound defense:

- Good tackling
- Aggressive, smart individual play
- Speed, especially on pass defense
- A well-coordinated defensive plan
- Personnel who compare physically with the opposition[40]

Furthermore, a feature of college football in the early days of the game and into the 1920s and beyond—unheard of today—is that the players played both offense and defense, most staying on the field for all sixty minutes of the game. There were very few player substitutions or time-outs, and often the only halt in play was to assess a penalty or due to a player injury. Joe Utay '08, who would be forever tied to Aggie football as captain of the 1907 team (as starting halfback and defensive back), was fond of recalling that for three seasons (1905, '06, and '07), he played every snap and all sixty minutes of every game except for five minutes of the 1906 TCU game.[41]

Against this background, the biggest game in the history of college football in the state of Texas to date would match the two coaches who had the greatest influence in establishing football at Texas A&M as well as gaining national recognition for the Southwest. Friends and fierce competitors, they

Early football at the A&M College of Texas was played on the main drill field across Military Walk in front of the Old Main, built in 1875–76 with twin towers known to cadets as "the bat roost." Notice the players wear no helmets and very little padding. (Source: author's collection)

had very different styles. While they both coached their teams to play to win with hard-hitting, aggressive football, Moran emphasized a smash-mouth form of the game. Bible was more the strategist, looking for holes in the defense for his generally undersized yet precocious offensive teams while demanding an aggressive defensive effort based on field position and capitalizing on turnovers. Many times, when backed up deep in their own territory, A&M punted on first downs just to move the ball out of harm's way, looking for a fumble by the receiving team—which often occurred.

And so the stage was set for the 1922 Dixie Classic.

CHAPTER 3

The Classic Game

While I am confident that the team will maintain its unbeaten record, I coached at A&M so long that I understand better than any outsider the value of the A. & M. spirit. I have never seen an A. and M. team quit—I never heard of one quitting. I brought Centre to Dallas with the information that they will have to fight for every inch of ground.

—Coach Charlie Moran,
January 1, 1922

I have never seen a squad in better spirits. They expect to show at the stadium a fighting machine that will be a credit to the State. A. and M. will adapt its style of play to the conditions that develop on the field.

—Coach Dana Bible,
January 1, 1922

The 1922 Dixie Classic was the brainchild of Joe Utay '08. Utay was familiar with the successful Dallas-sponsored championship baseball tournament known as the Dixie Series, and his intention was to create a postseason event to crown the collegiate football champion of the South. Like many in the South, Utay was painfully aware of the lack of attention and respect given to teams across the region. Hal Moseley '00, captain of the 1899 Aggie football team, assisted Utay and was very active in urging A&M to resume an annual game with the University of Texas in 1915 as well as play a role in the formation of the Southwest Conference.

Utay was no stranger to college football. As a scrappy 5′7″ 185-pound halfback, he played three years at Texas A&M. Following law school at Cumberland University in Lebanon, Tennessee, he coached at Holy Trinity College in Dallas before returning to A&M in 1912 as athletic director and coach of the freshman team during the tenure of Charlie Moran. After a season in College Station, Utay returned to his law practice and civic activities in Dallas as well as becoming a Southwest Conference football referee (1912–36).

In early 1918, Utay and Moseley (then the city manager of Dallas), along with a group of Texas Aggies in the Dallas A. and M. Club, petitioned Texas governor William P. Hobby for authorization to form a reserve army regiment to recruit, organize, and train for "duty over there." In July the War Department in Washington, D.C., approved the request of these citizen-soldiers for the activation of the 3rd Regiment of the Texas National Guard, known to all as "the A. and M. College Regiment." Utay was promoted to the rank of major in command of the regiment's 1st Battalion. Only the November 11, 1918, armistice ending World War I kept these Aggie citizen-soldiers, first trained in the Corps of Cadets, from being called to France. With the end of the war, Utay turned his attention back to his law firm, the promotion of the Dallas community, and football.[1]

In addition to the Dixie baseball tournament, Utay, apparently with assistance from the Dallas Chamber of Commerce, focused on organizing a much bigger event for football. Postseason bowl games were in their infancy. The first postseason college football game, viewed mostly as a novelty, was played at the Rose Bowl in Pasadena Tournament Park in California on January 1, 1902. Interest seems to have been high initially, yet soon waned after a robust Michigan squad from Lansing traveled west to roundly beat California favorite Stanford, 49–0. Discouraged by the outcome, the organizers abandoned future football games and for the next thirteen years instead held New Year's Day chariot races at the park, harking back to Roman times and inspired by the literary classic *Ben-Hur*. When interest in the dusty races waned and attendance plummeted, the organizing committee in 1915 opted to try football again, with another game at the Rose Bowl on January 1, 1916. This game featured West Coast favorite Washington State against the East's Brown University. State prevailed, 14–0. The Rose Bowl games continued as an annual tradition after that. Their first competition came not from Dallas but from the Fort Worth Classic on January 1, 1921, recognized as the second postseason football bowl game in the nation.[2]

Promoters of the Fort Worth Classic wanted to match a local team, TCU, with a nationally recognized team. The most talked-about non–Ivy League football team was from Centre College, a small school in Danville, Kentucky. The Colonels' reputation caught the attention of the organizers. Over a four-season period from 1917 to 1920, Centre had compiled a record of 28–3, shutting out twenty of its thirty-one opponents during that period and amassing 1,432 points to their opponents' 104. TCU's record for the same

College Bowl History, 1902–1922

Date	Bowl	Teams	
Jan. 1, 1902	Rose	Michigan 49	Stanford 0
Jan. 1, 1916	Rose	Washington State 14	Brown 0
Jan. 1, 1917	Rose	Oregon 14	Pennsylvania 0
Jan. 1, 1918	Rose	Mare Island Marines 19	Camp Lewis 0
Jan. 1, 1919	Rose	Great Lakes 17	Mare Island Marines 0
Jan. 1, 1920	Rose	Harvard 7	Oregon 6
Jan. 1, 1921	Rose	California 28	Ohio State 0
Jan. 1, 1921	Fort Worth Classic	Centre 63	TCU 7
Dec. 26, 1921	Christmas Bowl	Centre 38	Arizona 0
Jan. 2, 1922	Dixie Classic	Texas A&M 22	Centre 14
Jan. 2, 1922	Rose	Washington & Jefferson 0	California 0

period was 22 wins and 12 losses, yet the 1920 Frogs' season was a perfect 9–0. Notwithstanding, promoters were confident the game would be a splendid affair, and it was. The Colonels, billed in the media as the "Wonder Team," lived up to their reputation and defeated a bewildered TCU, 63–7. This was the first and last year of the Fort Worth Classic. Few are aware that the trip to Fort Worth was the first of three bowl games the Colonels would play in a twelve-month period. Centre, in fact, played in the second, third, and fourth bowl games ever organized.[3]

In November 1921 the Colonels were offered a contract to play in the New Year's Day 1922 Rose Bowl but declined because they had committed to the upstart Christmas Bowl, scheduled on December 26, 1921, in San Diego. Billed as an East-West postseason match to compete with the Rose Bowl, Centre was pitted against the Arizona Wildcats, whom they dispatched with ease, 38–0.

In hindsight, it is uncertain whether the Rose Bowl wanted an exclusive commitment from Centre College. The Colonels, always looking for a good match, almost certainly could have traveled 100 miles up the coast to play on New Year's Day, five days after their easy defeat of Arizona. However, Moran's focus was on beating Texas A&M in Dallas. So instead of traveling north to Pasadena, the Colonels boarded a special reserved first-class Pullman train car for the 1,400-mile trip eastward to Texas, departing San Diego on the Santa Fe Railroad at 12:01 a.m., December 27, and, after a long delay, arriving in Dallas at 2:30 p.m. on December 30. At that moment the "Wonder Team" was hailed as the undisputed number-one team in the country.[4]

In an era before broadcast sports media, newspaper sportswriters dominated the stories of football across the nation. In the reporting about Centre's 38–0 victory after the Arizona game, with the Wildcats having surrendered only 30 points all season, the reputation of "America's greatest team" was embellished at every turn and received dramatic coverage—something the Texas Aggies and their fans were well aware of. The team from Tucson had only six first downs and never remotely threatened the Colonels. This accounting, only days before the Dallas game, was surely of concern to Coach Bible and the Aggies:

> **Bo and Mates Take Wildness out of Wildcats**
>
> Centre won 38–0. Field sloppy. Weather raining. On a fast [dry] gridiron, in my humble estimation, Centre could have made it 75–0.
>
> Arizona had no business in the same park with the famous Kentucky Colonels. They were outclassed from the start. Of all the Western champions, only California could have stood toe to toe with Centre yesterday. So closely would they have been matched that the breaks of luck may have decided the battle.
>
> Sockless for the reason that wet woolens may have cut down in his speed, Bo McMillin packed the ball the majority of times that it was in the Colonels' possession, and he lived up to all of his advance notices. He was one Eastern satellite brought West who lived up to predictions.
>
> Bo skidded all over the soggy field in a manner that dazzled. He broke loose continuously for 20 and 30 yard runs. His slippery clothing made him even more elusive and difficult to tackle. Like an eel was Bo. There was no stopping the stalwart Kentuckian. He snapped out his signals and then executed deeds of daring back of the stone wall of his line. His passing was brilliant, and he was successful even though he was throwing a slippery ball.
>
> The teaming of McMillin with Red Roberts leading the way provided a force that Arizona was unable to stop. Red served as a Roman shield for McMillin. Roberts roved around the field, first

Texas A&M–Centre College Records, 1917–1921

	Texas A&M	Centre College
1917	8–0–0	7–1–0
1918	6–1–0*	4–0–0***
1919	10–0–0	9–0–0
1920	6–1–1	8–2–0
1921	5–1–2**	8–0–0**
Totals	35–3–3	36–3–0

*Bible in US Army in France
**Record prior to Dixie Classic
***Reduced wartime schedule

> playing end, then tackle and then at full [back] when brought into the backfield to serve as a battering ram for Bo, or to carry the ball when a sure gain was needed.
>
> Centre showed speed and dash in the attack, before which Arizona was helpless. The Kentuckians marched down the field almost at will. Through tackle and around ends, the heavy Centre men assaulted their lighter foe for consistent gains. Generally it was McMillin you found breaking loose. Sometimes Bartlett, Armstrong, Tanner, Snowday, Murphy, or Covington. Centre just had too many horses, too much talent.
>
> Centre is unquestionably the greatest college football team to ever come out of the East to play the West—Centre revealed an amazing speed and power which the West can never forget.[5]

The article on Centre's victory and dominating style constituted virtually all of the advance information available in a time before scouting reports and advance game film. However, the five-season game record of the two teams provided more evidence of a worthy matchup between the Aggies and Colonels.

THE ROAD TO DALLAS

The rise of Centre College football to national prominence began in the fall of 1915 at North Side High School in Fort Worth, Texas. Player development and initial coaching at North Side were orchestrated by a 1907 Centre College graduate, Coach Robert Lee Myers, affectionately called "Chief" by his players. He was the man, noted an expert on Centre College history, who "made it all happen." While a college student, Myers had gone out for the Colonels' team one year, but did not play very much. He loved the game, but upon graduation was called home to Chicago to work in the family entertainment business. His dream was to help his little college build a championship team. To do so he needed training and experience. So he became a dedicated student of the game, spending any extra time in the fall at University of Chicago practices to watch what famed coach Amos Alonzo Stagg was doing to prepare his team. Myers attended every football clinic advertised and conducted by coaches, including Pop Warner, coach of the Carlisle Indians. Five years after returning to Chicago, Myers learned of an open high school position in Fort Worth to teach English and coach football. He applied and in 1912 was hired at North Side High School.[6]

Shortly after arriving, Myers had an encounter with a young student, Alvin Nugent McMillin, who had dropped out of school to help his family after his father died. Myers mentored the boy and told him he could get assistance and should return to school. And since Myers was the coach, he could play football. The two joined over the next few years to bring acclaim to themselves and their schools. "Bo," as Alvin was known to his friends and soon the news media, would be the nucleus and natural leader of a very talented group of Fort Worth players, and Myers provided the coaching and inspiration to win. Coach Myers's vision was to prepare a core of talented players to be the seeds of a future winning program at Centre. Few of the boys had ever traveled outside of Texas, and so Chief regularly told them about his alma mater in Kentucky, and covered the walls of the dressing room with slogans: "BELIEVE! ACHIEVE! SUCCEED!" But first he had to build the North Side Steers into a Texas football powerhouse. In the fall of 1915, North Side won nearly every game, losing only the final game for the state championship to the Austin Maroons at the University of Texas stadium on the Austin campus.[7]

While still coaching at North Side, Myers began to make arrangements to enroll his Texas boys in Centre. An initial group of nine Fort Worth football players (over a three-year period there would be a total of twelve) would travel nine hundred miles to the small community of Danville, Kentucky, for their next challenge. In that first group were Matty Bell, Bob Mathis, Red Weaver, Bo McMillin, Thad McDonnell, Bill James, Sully Montgomery, Bill Boswell, and Reuben McMillin. But in August 1916, Myers's plan hit a snag when it was discovered that three of his key players, Bo, Red, and

Thad, did not have enough high school credits to enter college. Unfazed, Chief found local homes and jobs in Danville for the boys and enrolled the trio in the local Somerset High School. The Texans helped the Somerset team, known as the "Briar Jumpers," dominate Kentucky high school football, playing for a scoreless tie in the state championship game in Lexington—the second state championship appearance by the trio in as many years. In addition to the Texans from Fort Worth, seven of the Briar Jumpers enrolled at Centre. Watching from Chicago (where he had briefly returned to work with the family business), Myers waited for an opportunity to return to Danville. One presented itself in mid-1917, when Coach Orville Littick resigned to go to Beloit College. In the same article that reported Littick's departure, it was confirmed that Myers would take over the Colonels' football program. Any question that the Chief had had a long-term plan is answered by the fact that the starting 1917 lineup had five players from Fort Worth's North Side: quarterback Bo McMillin, fullback Bob Mathis, right guard Reuben McMillin, center Red Weaver, and left end Matty Bell. Another player who could claim a bit of a Texas connection was the right halfback, Tom Moran, son of Charlie, yet he was listed as hailing from his family's hometown, Horse Cave, Kentucky.[8]

UNCLE CHARLIE

To this day, the arrival of Coach Moran at Centre College is fodder for the legend of a man who had already made his mark at Texas A&M, winning 76 percent of his games. Following his departure from A&M in December 1914, he coached briefly for the Carlisle Indians, was an umpire for the Southern Baseball Association, and in late 1916 began a second career as a baseball umpire in the National League. The events that placed Moran at the helm of the Colonels were chronicled by Dr. Robert W. Robertson in *The Wonder Team:*

> A somewhat gruff looking man strolled out onto the practice field on Monday October 22, 1917 and introduced himself to the Chief. Known as Uncle Charlie, Moran had a son, Tom, on the team, and asked if he could watch the practice. The Chief knew Moran, because he had a very successful coaching career at Texas A&M from 1909–1914, years that overlapped with Myers's tenure in Fort Worth. Moran was 39 years old and had just begun a career as a

National League professional baseball umpire during the just-ended 1917 season.

He was an offensive genius and offered some tips to the Chief about how he may want to open up his attack. Moran said that since the baseball season was over, he'd be happy to help out with the team for the rest of the season. And—he'd do it for nothing. No salary. He'd just volunteer his time. Before the afternoon was over, Centre had a new football coach.[9]

While there was some concern among the older team members, the Chief agreed with the change, making it clear he wanted the team to go to the next competitive level and that Moran was the man to be head coach. To continue his longtime connection with the Centre program, Myers would remain as athletic director and an active assistant coach. Furthermore, the Chief had the ear of the college administration, was critical to future player recruiting, and was a mentor to many of the players—Myers would be a surrogate father for Bo for a decade. Uncle Charlie and the Chief jointly drafted a plan of action: first, become and continue as undisputed champions of

Coach Charlie Moran and his son Tom at Centre College in 1921. (Source: Centre College Special Collections and Archives)

college football in Kentucky; second, schedule games with teams from larger universities to gain more recognition; third, maintain aggressive player recruiting; and then become the champions of the East and vie for the national championship. Step one was to prepare the Colonels for the 1917 season. They recorded an 8–1 season that year, scoring 247 points and allowing only 6 points in their lone loss, to DePauw.[10]

Like all other athletic programs around the country, sports events were greatly curtailed after the April 1917 declaration of war on Germany and the Axis Powers. And like other institutions, staff, players, and faculty were soon in uniform for duty "over there." The disruption, with Centre playing only four local games in Danville in 1918, was further impacted by the deadly October 1918 influenza outbreak that shut down all campus activities, sports programs, and travel across the country. With the end of the war in November, returning players were given an extra year of eligibility due to the war.[11]

Thirteen of the twenty Centre players who lettered in 1918 returned in 1919. Postwar recruiting across Kentucky and the nation was fierce, yet the Colonels had made a name for themselves in the region and picked up a number of key players. The core players of the team, much like the Texas Aggies during the same period, numbered only about eighteen to twenty each season through the mid-1920s. Players were expected to routinely play both offense and defense; there were no multiple substitutions or special teams. Bo was famously quoted as saying, "Uncle Charlie expected you to play the whole game. You had to get almost killed before he'd take you out." Centre expanded its fall schedule from eight games in 1917 to nine games in 1919 and ten games in 1920. The 1919 season added "big schools" Virginia, Indiana, and West Virginia, resulting in an undefeated season record of 9–0. Moran felt the key game of 1919 was the 14–6 win over the West Virginia Mountaineers, followed by increased media attention. Moran and Centre received nationwide attention when it was reported that the team held a prayer at halftime, with the coach telling a reporter, "It's hard to beat a praying team." As a result, the team soon acquired the sobriquet "Prayin' Colonels."[12]

In defeat, West Virginia fans and some media questioned how a small college (Centre had a student body of 193; over 10 percent of the students were on the football team) could play so well, and they quickly assumed there must be a bunch of last-minute, walk-on ringers. There were reports that players Weaver, Roberts, and Murphy were not "real" students. In fact, the three alleged ringers had been enrolled for two continuous years; with the players' academic transcripts in hand, administration officials demanded an apology, backing the coach and the team. Much like the attacks by UT on Moran in 1911, West Virginia partisans hoped to discredit him and Centre. This time it did not work. West Virginia had simply been outcoached and outplayed.[13]

The bigger question at the end of the 1919 season was who was the number-one team in the nation. With no formal rankings or national polls, five teams claimed a share of the title: Texas A&M at 10–0, Notre Dame at 9–0, Centre at 9–0, Harvard at 9–0–1, and Tulsa at 8–0–1. However, the more newsworthy item in Danville was the fact that the Colonels were the only team in the country to place three players on the famed Walter Camp's 1919 All-American team: quarterback Bo McMillin, halfback Red Roberts, and center Red Weaver. This was big news in the South. Since 1900, only one other southern football player, Bill Fincher of Georgia Tech, had been named to the prestigious postseason list. And collegiate football across Texas and the South was completely ignored by the East Coast–dominated sports media.[14]

The big test for Centre came in 1920 when Harvard, Virginia Polytechnic Institute, and Georgia Tech were scheduled. The first test would be Harvard in Cambridge on October 23, 1920. The Prayin' Colonels entered the contest with a 22-game undefeated run over four seasons. The Myers-Moran plan to play the big schools had come to fruition. The Colonels, for only the first time between 1917 and 1924, lost two games back to back: a 14–31 defeat by Harvard followed by a rare shutout by Georgia Tech in Atlanta, 0–24. Nevertheless, the nationwide publicity for Centre only helped fuel the expectations for the 1921 Harvard-Centre rematch. Nor was Moran's success lost on his friends in College Station, as the Texas A&M *Alumni Quarterly* noted his team had "decisively defeated the best teams of the North and East," and the front cover of the *Texas Aggie* tabloid extended congratulations to Moran for being named to the Coaches Hall of Fame. Moran was fondly remembered in Aggieland with headlines such as "A. and M. Roots as Charlie Licks Them." The much-hyped Harvard game met all expectations, with Bo breaking away to score the only touchdown in a 6–0 victory over Harvard, to cap off a perfect 8–0 regular season going into the 1921 San Diego Christmas Bowl. Headlines about the Centre victory, like this one in the *Augusta Herald*, electrified the South: "Harvard Is Humbled by a Southern Football Team." Teams across the South gained long overdue attention. The clamor for the Centre Colonels to be crowned the champions of the nation only grew in volume.[15]

Sam Houston Sanders '22 was a 130-pound halfback and star track and field athlete. Sammy returned the opening kickoff in the Dixie Classic. (Source: Cushing Memorial Library and Archives)

BIBLE'S BUNCH

Coach Bible and many of the 1917 championship team were back in College Station in 1919 following service during the war. Bible had missed the 1918 season while in France, yet that year assistant Tubby Graves guided the team to a 6–1 record, with a lone loss to Texas, 0–7. While the coach was concerned about a strong defense, much to his surprise the Aggies were able to field a lethal pair of veteran running backs: Jack Mahan, "Mr. Inside," and "Little Hig" Higginbotham, "Mr. Outside." Both Jack and Hig earned All-SWC recognition. Their new young players, G. W. Martin, C. R. Drake, and Cap Murrah, helped fill out the roster. Players during this era continued to play on both sides of the ball for sixty minutes, resulting in a growing number of injuries, and Mahan, Arthur Knickerbocker, and Martin were sidelined for a time. In 1919, Bible's stress on field position and an unbending defense resulted in his second perfect 10–0 record: undefeated, untied, and unscored upon, racking up 275 points to 0. The 1919 season was capped with a 7–0 win against Texas, the third straight win over the Longhorns at Kyle Field since 1915. The winning continued into the 1920 season, with a lone 0–0 tie with LSU and a 25-game winning record on the eve of the 1921 Thanksgiving game with undefeated and untied Texas at Austin. The Aggies scored a field goal to take the lead, but in the closing moments of the game Texas scored, leaving no time for A&M to strike back; Texas won 7–3 and captured the first Southwest Conference championship.

"You can understand why it was such a bitter defeat," Bible recalled, "and it was compounded by the loss coming so late in the game." A half century later, he noted, "That loss was the hardest to take of my coaching career."[16]

"GOOD-BYE TO TEXAS UNIVERSITY"

If there was any doubt why the University of Texas was A&M's archrival, there is no better indicator than the choice of the Aggie fight song, adopted in 1920–21 and still used to this day, even though the University of Texas is no longer on the Aggies' annual fall schedule. The rivalry dated from the mid-1890s and by 1910 had heated up to an annual match that was followed across the state. For years the students and fans exchanged chants, yells, and brief songs, all intended to fire up the teams. While Texas A&M had more than fifty different game yells, as of 1920 they still had no official fight song; over more than a decade, numerous songs and chants had been considered, but none survived. In late 1918, however, after sophomore cadet

James V. "Pinky" Wilson '20 had enlisted in the US Marine Corps and was shipped to France, he penned the first draft of a ballad memorializing the annual scrap between the Aggies and the Longhorns. He was inspired by his memories of the yells, spirit, and excitement of the 1917 Thanksgiving game, and came up with what was initially intended to be a ballad sung to the tune of a popular barbershop song, "Coney Island Baby."

Returning to A&M in the fall of 1919, Wilson and his musical group, the Cast Iron Quartet, introduced the song at a local theater during intermission. Shortly thereafter Wilson was approached by the yell leaders and cadets to "jazz up" the song for a possible entry as the college's fight song, and he agreed. It seems that "Good-bye to Texas University," not yet officially called the "Aggie War Hymn," was sung in late 1920 at the Texas game.[17] The single verse was written down for publication as sheet music with the help of George Fairleigh, the Aggie band director, and formally introduced on Thanksgiving 1921 under the title "The Battle Hymn of A&M: Good-bye to Texas U." Years later, Wilson wrote a second verse, telling me in 1976, "I think it's better, but the Aggies will never sing it." Over the years, sheet music and publications have reversed the verses, but there is only one "first" verse that is still sung as the "Aggie War Hymn" to this day:

Hullabaloo, Caneck! Caneck!
Hullabaloo, Caneck! Caneck!
Good-bye to Texas University,
So long to the orange and the white.
Good luck to the dear old Texas Aggies,
They are the boys who show the real old fight.
The eyes of Texas are upon you,
That is the song they sing so well—
So, good-bye to Texas University
We're going to beat you all to—
Chig-gar-roo-gar-rem!
Chig-gar-roo-gar-rem!
Rough! Tough!
Real Stuff! Texas A&M![18]

There was little doubt that the Aggies and the Longhorns would again go head-to-head in 1921. Both teams had seasoned players and what appeared to be a shot to compete for the conference championship. However, the two teams' schedules gave A&M a clearer path to the title, since A&M

played five conference opponents and Texas only two: Rice and Texas A&M. It is not certain when Joe Utay tapped the Aggies to host the first Dixie Classic, although the invitation was issued to Bible prior to the end of the 1921 season. The University of Texas team was heralded by the sports media to be the best ever fielded by the Longhorns after their shutout victories (scoring 104 points against their opponents' zero) in their first three games. However, this sentiment soon waned after Texas lost to Vanderbilt at Fair Park in Dallas, 20–0.[19]

At this point in the season the Aggies were 5–1 after a narrow loss to non-conference LSU. It was expected A&M would roll past Rice and Texas in their final two games and end with an 7–1 record and the SWC crown. If this scenario had played out, the Aggies and the Colonels would have had 35 wins each for the five seasons from 1917 through 1921 (and each team would have had only 3 losses). They were primed for their January New Year's match in Dallas. However, the Aggies ended the season with ties against Rice, 7–7, and Texas, 0–0. Nevertheless, A&M, "by common consent," captured the SWC title.[20] With that, the Dixie Classic matchup was set, and the teams and fans began their final preparations.

THE BIG EVENT

Impressed with the success of the Rose Bowl in Pasadena, California, and the upstart Fort Worth Classic, Joe Utay determined there was a great opportunity to promote football in Texas as well as to highlight his hometown, Dallas. Planning for the postseason game (this was long before they were routinely called "bowl games") began in September 1921. Dallas generally had good weather in early January, so Utay selected the Fair Park grounds for the Monday, January 2 kickoff. Fully aware of the Rose Bowl's selection process, Utay worked to confirm the best team in the nation to play the Southwest champion, which was yet to be crowned.[21]

Utay's first choice was Penn State, but in mid-November, when the Nittany Lions tied Harvard, 21–21, he turned his attention to courting Alfred Earle "Greasy" Neale, coach of the Presidents of Washington and Jefferson College, located in Washington, Pennsylvania. The Presidents seemed to be on track to be the champions of the East, with a 10–0 record. This would have been a great matchup with the Aggies, who, going into their last two games with Rice and Texas, had only one non-conference loss, to LSU, and Neale agreed. But by signing W&J, Utay had scooped the Rose Bowl committee, who quickly appealed to him to allow them to match W&J with the

University of California, the champs of the West. Acknowledging that the Rose Bowl was "the world series of football," Utay relented and released W&J from the contract so that they could play Cal in Pasadena (that game would end in a 0–0 tie). Then he began the search for a new opponent.[22]

Just four weeks away from kickoff of the Dixie Classic, Utay, a one-man search committee, scrambled to sign an opponent. Reflecting on the tremendous military record of the Fightin' Texas Aggies during the war and the strong patriotism of the postwar environment, Utay next sent a telegram and express letter to the United States Military Academy at West Point. The matchup of the two leading military colleges in the nation would surely guarantee a successful first game, he thought. But his hopes were cut short by a letter from the academy superintendent, General Douglas MacArthur, on December 9, 1921, stating, "It will be impossible for the football team to accept the invitation. . . . The policy of the War Department does not permit . . . such an extensive trip."[23] This would not be the last time that the former students and officers of Texas A&M would cross paths with General MacArthur. But since MacArthur had refused, Joe kept looking.

In the era before "big football" at the larger state institutions, small private colleges (with enrollments under 700 students) had tremendously successful teams. The football media thrived on stories of such "giant-killer" teams. In December 1921, sports headlines nationwide were filled with the success of a little college team in Danville, Kentucky. Indeed, the only sports figures of prominence in the fall of 1921 who received more attention than Bo and the Prayin' Colonels were Babe Ruth, Ty Cobb, and Jack Dempsey. The Centre College Colonels, in only a few short seasons, had amassed a very impressive record under Utay's old friend Coach Moran and garnered extensive media coverage. Centre's 1921 season ended with an 8–0 record, the Colonels giving up only 6 points while scoring 307 points. This included a major victory over Harvard, breaking the Crimson's 25-game winning streak, which dated back three seasons. After conferring with A&M president William Bizzell to explain the situation with the Rose Bowl and the declined offer to West Point, Joe Utay contacted his old friend Coach Moran to arrange a matchup between the Colonels and the Aggies in Dallas. Uncle Charlie agreed at once. He seemed unconcerned by the short time between the Colonels' bowl game in San Diego and the proposed new game; nor did he seem worried about the lengthy travel that would be required. His strong previous ties to the state of Texas, along with those of a number of his players, persuaded him to welcome the chance to play—and beat—the college that had fired him in 1914. Utay apparently did not mention to

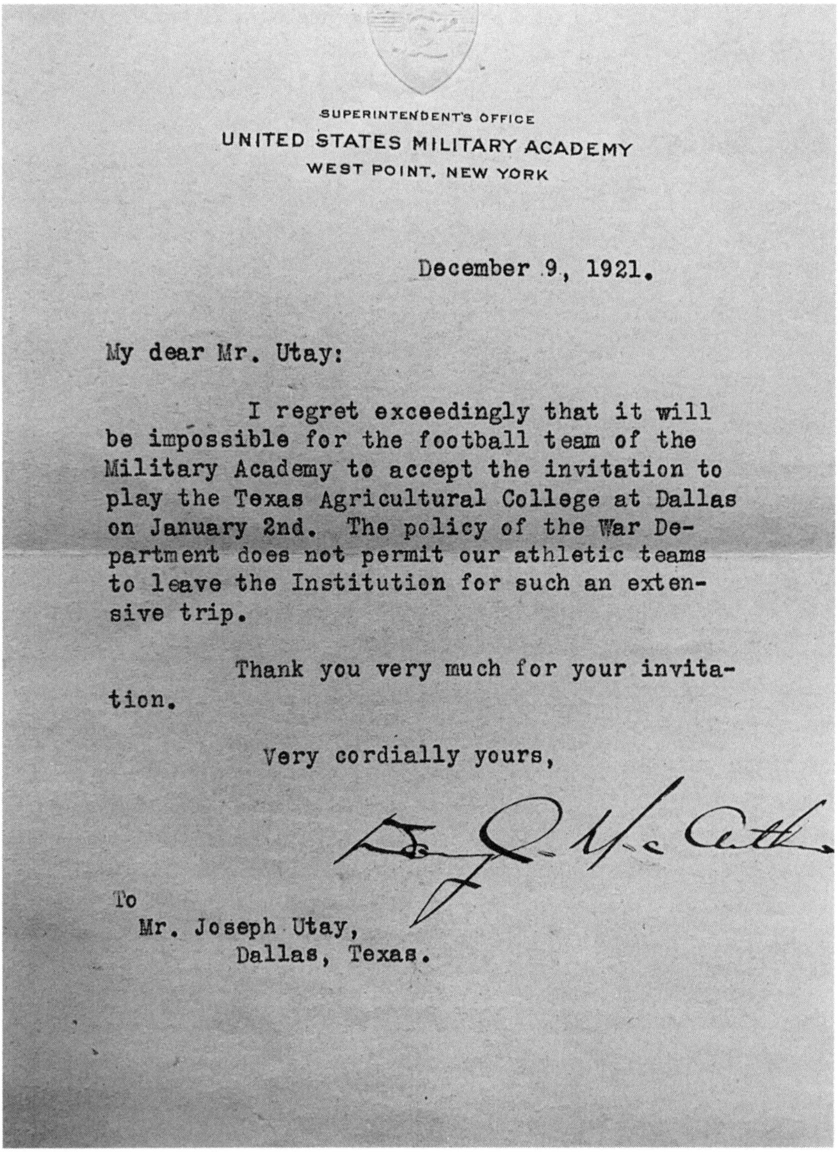

SUPERINTENDENT'S OFFICE
UNITED STATES MILITARY ACADEMY
WEST POINT, NEW YORK

December 9, 1921.

My dear Mr. Utay:

I regret exceedingly that it will be impossible for the football team of the Military Academy to accept the invitation to play the Texas Agricultural College at Dallas on January 2nd. The policy of the War Department does not permit our athletic teams to leave the Institution for such an extensive trip.

Thank you very much for your invitation.

Very cordially yours,

To
Mr. Joseph Utay,
Dallas, Texas.

After Washington and Jefferson College were released to go to the Rose Bowl, Joe Utay attempted to schedule West Point for the Dixie Classic, but he was turned down by Brigadier General Douglas MacArthur only three weeks before the scheduled kickoff. (Source: Cushing Memorial Library and Archives)

Moran that Centre College was the third-choice team to play the Aggies in the Classic.[24]

THE RED CARPET

In spite of the fact that the Colonels' train was twenty-two hours late arriving at the Dallas Union Terminal on December 30, they received a grand welcome. The team was met by a score of Kentucky and Centre College alumni who paraded the team to the Adolphus Hotel in a "fleet of high-powered cars" decked out in gold and white ribbons. The grand Adolphus Hotel, with more than 1,000 guest rooms, was possibly the most opulent hotel west of the Mississippi River. It had been built in 1911 by the founder of Anheuser-Busch, Adolphus Busch of St. Louis. At twenty-two stories, it was the tallest building in Texas for over a decade before being dwarfed by the Magnolia Petroleum Company building. With wall-to-wall plush carpet, vaulted ceilings, grand ballrooms, and fine dining facilities, the hotel was the center of social, business, and political activities in Texas for over three decades.

As soon as they checked in, the team changed into their uniforms and hustled out to the fairgrounds for a workout. Following practice, the Texas A&M alumni held a reception for both squads, ending abruptly with the team curfew at 10:00 p.m. The Centre College men had been traveling more or less constantly since December 16, and following their six-day train trip to California they had a week of festivities and parades prior to the San Diego Christmas Bowl. Now they were in Dallas at the end of another long rail journey, and were almost certainly fatigued.[25]

Coach Bible and the Aggies had arrived in Dallas the day before, on Thursday, December 29, and settled into their headquarters at the old Holy Trinity College, recently renamed Dallas University. Bible had selected the college as his pregame camp, most likely with the assistance of Joe Utay, because it was a spartan, no-frills location. Though he agreed to allow his team to participate in the December 30 reception, Bible was not interested in dinners, parades, or festivities and sought out an isolated spot in order to concentrate on game preparation. He had scouted the Centre team by talking with coaches who had played the Colonels during the season; sharing such information was not unusual in the period before game film. Bible started a two-a-day practice routine with workouts after breakfast followed by a "chalk talk" and lunch, a brief rest, and a full daily scrimmage session primarily devoted to defense. In one of the hard-hitting practices, star running back Floyd "Buck" Buckner was injured and knocked out of the lineup.[26]

Bible's lifelong approach to football, chronicled in his bestselling book, *Championship Football,* was straightforward:

> There is no easy way to play football. It isn't that kind of game. It is a hard game for hardy characters—for boys who are tough in body and spirit. Desire, determination, spirit, the will to win, the love of contact—call it what you like; it still can cover a multitude of sins in a football game. The player who fairly explodes in his eagerness to slam an opponent to the turf is more likely to excel over a mechanically superior opponent who lacks that urge. A team's success or failure in any particular game may defy generalization, certain components will make or break it over the long pull. These components are called by different names—let's call them the Five S's: Spirit, Speed, Skill, Size, and Savvy.[27]

In Centre College, the Texas Aggies were facing a challenge that would require all the Five S's.

Going into the game, the Aggies were dealing with a number of injuries from the last two 1921 regular-season games with Rice and Texas. Furthermore, as the media reported numerous times, the eighteen Aggie players were "heavily" outweighed by 10–20 pounds, and according to Coach Bible, the "Colonels were figured a 20-point favorite." A week earlier the Colonels had embarrassed a powerful Arizona team, their fourteenth straight victory. The *Dallas Morning News* on the day of the game carried the headline "Centre Is Favorite to Win Battle." And while the key to Bible's game plan was to concentrate on defense, he remarked, "I know the spectators will look for us to play a defensive game. But all our games this year were not won by defensive play. A&M will adapt its style of play to the conditions that develop on the field. I have never seen a squad in better spirits on the eve of a big game." One paper reported that "Moran's men reveled while Aggies slept" during the New Year's celebrations in downtown Dallas. True to his intentions, Coach Bible's team remained in the old student dormitories at Dallas University. He did, however, permit them to attend the "Get Together" banquet held on Sunday evening at the Oriental Hotel. The event was hosted by the Dallas A&M Club and Dallas Chamber of

Commerce for both teams. Marion Church '08 presided as toastmaster and Mayor S. R. Aldredge and Dr. William Bizzell, president of Texas A&M, gave welcoming remarks.[28]

By the early 1920s, football had become a major national phenomenon rivaled only by baseball. The emerging scale of the game demanded organization, coordination, and clear direction. The pregame pageantry so routine today, with such programs as Saturday morning's *Game Day* on ESPN, alumni homecoming events, and, in the case of the Texas Aggies, midnight yell practice, has its roots in the dynamic social aspects of the game begun in this golden age of college football and the excitement of the Roaring Twenties. Football was at once a sport and a major social event. And as the Centre College team would soon demonstrate, what could be more "social" than a grand, pregame wedding of a heralded All-American football player and his high school sweetheart?[29]

PREGAME WEDDING

The morning of Monday, January 2, 1922, was cool, breezy, and clear in Dallas. The pregame routines for the two teams would be as drastically different as could be imagined. Bo McMillin had agreed weeks earlier with his high school sweetheart and fiancée, Maud Marie Miers, to January 2 as their wedding day, long before the Dixie Classic game date was confirmed for Centre. After conferring with the Chief and Coach Moran, they decided to go ahead with the planned nuptials; all parties were aware that Bo's wedding was factored in from the outset.

Since arriving in Dallas, twenty-seven-year-old Bo had missed all the practices, yet attended all the dinners and receptions. His time up until the morning of the game had been spent in Fort Worth with both his family and that of his wife-to-be. The pregame routine for the Colonels was also altered. The team was up very early to dress and go to Union Station to take the train westward to Fort Worth for the 9:00 a.m. wedding and high Mass at All Saints Catholic Church.

Bo's best man was Thad McDonnell, and groomsmen were Red Roberts, Bill James, Ben Cregor, Norris "Army" Armstrong, and Tom Moran. Following the ceremony, all were rushed back to Dallas by car to the Adolphus Hotel for a tremendous feast at the lavish post-wedding brunch. Uncle Charlie was overheard reminding the players, "Slow down on the eating, we have a big game in a few hours."[30] After they ate, the Colonels were hustled into a caravan of private cars, headed for Fair Park.

Across town, Coach Bible had allowed the Aggies to sleep in until the 9:00 a.m. required breakfast in the spartan college dining hall. This was followed by an extensive skull session and review of all possible scenarios. The team went out on the practice field to line up and review one last time their defensive positions and assignments. Bible's primary strategy was to control the defensive side of the ball and shut down the high-powered Centre offense. Shortly after noon the Aggies dressed in their game uniforms and quietly boarded two old school buses.

Though "red and white" had slowly emerged as the Aggie colors, the football uniforms remained a very drab black and gray with horizontal stripes. Numbers, still considered optional, were on the back of the jerseys. Cleated shoes were commonly used, worn with knee-high, striped socks, and the helmet was a lightweight, one-inch thick padded leather covering with no face guard. As the cadets prepared for pregame drills, the Colonels were exiting the music and fanfare of the Adolphus wedding brunch and hustling into a caravan of private cars, headed for Fair Park.

The crowd that day at Fair Park was estimated to be nearly twelve thousand. While there was a large contingent of Kentuckians to support the Colonels, the vast majority were backing the Aggies. However, all attention was on Centre and their stars. Bo and his new wife, Maud, led the team onto the field arm in arm, and she sat on the team bench the entire game.

The sports media, including the local sportswriters, who were partial to Texas teams, had already placed odds on the Colonels, who were 4–1 favorites over A&M. The Aggies were not even given an outside chance to win, though some sportswriters did caution that the Aggies shouldn't be counted out. Still, Centre entered the game undefeated, having outscored their opponents by 314 to 6. But as one observer wisely noted, "games are won on the field, and not in the newspaper."[31]

Star A&M halfback Sammy Sanders and the team were as amazed as their fans with their first look at the foe: "When they came on the field, the Centre players were putting on a show. The passers were throwing left and right-handed, and the punters were kicking with either leg. Meantime, our punter's kicks into the wind were flying back over his head. This added to the pressure on us, and to the onlookers it must have looked like we were outclassed in ability."[32]

One interesting feature of the Dixie Classic was that some fifteen players, divided between the two teams, were from the Dallas–Fort Worth area. Chief Myers's boys from North Side High School in Fort Worth alone accounted for seven players on the Centre squad. The Aggies from the local area included Arthur Dieterich, guard; L. S. "Tiny" Keen, tackle; W. E. "Ted" Winn, tackle; and R. V. "Crack" DuBois, center.[33]

WIRE-TO-WIRE AND PLAY-BY-PLAY

In an era before nationwide radio and television broadcasts, direct, continuous telegram and telephone lines were operated by an entrepreneurial Texas A&M cadet, David J. "Mike" Finn '21, beginning with the October 8, 1920, game between A&M and SMU at Fair Park in Dallas. This bold project involved obtaining a telephone lease and rights for a direct, uninterrupted line to the A&M campus. This was the first time this was attempted at the college, contrary to later reports of a similar hookup in the fall of 1922. Finn arranged to use the college's stock-judging pavilion, where he set up amplifiers and a layout of a football field on the arena floor to track the play-by-play action. Finn, with the assistance of William "Doc" Tolson '23, was on the receiving end of the plays, and cadets Othman C. Thompson '22 and Arthur C. Keith '22 were in Dallas, sending the transmission of game action. Finn's admission charge for the event was 35 cents, and his sales pitch was "Why go to Dallas for the game, when you can hear it called play for play at the Pavilion?" The "reports" and commentary on the game were provided by former student William B. "Bean" Harkrider '20. The "telegrammed" game, a 3–0 victory by A&M over SMU, was a big success in the Pavilion, attended by both President Bizzell and Dean of Engineering J. C. Nagle, who commented to Finn, "[We] must commend your enterprise." This first success resulted in similar coverage of the Texas A&M–Oklahoma A&M contest from Stillwater, another Aggie victory (35–0), though Finn raised the entry fee to 50 cents to help cover the total expenses of $150. This set the stage to "broadcast" games in the fall of 1921.[34]

In advance of the 1921 game with Texas, the play-by-play broadcast was moved to the main telephone/telegraph office in the Wallace Building in downtown Bryan, Texas. Earlier in the 1921 season, Aggie cadets Tolson, Lewis "B" Wilson '17, and Harry M. Saunders '22 had set up an "experimental station" with the call sign 5YA, using surplus US Army Signal Corps equipment left on campus after World War I training. The transmitter used three 5-watt tubes with a total output of approximately 175 watts. They rigged up a telegraph line between Kyle Field and the Electrical Engineering building, a half-mile across campus, with a line to Austin to test the system and to transmit the 1921 A&M–Texas Thanksgiving game, which

The 1922 Dixie Classic Pregame Lineup

Texas A&M	Weight	Position	Weight	Centre College
Richard O. "Puny" Wilson	180	Left end	210	James B. "Red" Roberts
W. E. "Ted" Winn	166	Left tackle	183	Minos T. "Cajun" Gordy
W. E. "Cap" Murrah	205	Left guard	203	George P. "Buck" Jones
H. V. "Crack" DuBois	153	Center	175	Edwin Kubale
A. F. Dieterich	180	Right guard	177	William P. Shadoan
R. L. "Bob" Carruthers	163	Right tackle	180	Ben W. "Baldy" Cregor
A. J. "Jack" Evans	175	Right end	175	William N. James
A. B. "Bugs" Morris	147	Quarterback	165	Alvin N. "Bo" McMillin
Tom L. Miller*	163	Left half	178	Terry Snoddy
Sammy H. Sanders	130	Right half	155	Norris "Army" Armstrong**
W. C. "Heine" Weir **	156	Fullback	157	Tom Bartlett

*Punter
**Captain
Weights as listed in game-day program.
Additional players:
Texas A&M: W. G. "Bill" McMillan; T. F. "Tuffy" Wendt; Ben B. Beesley; William D. "Bull" Johnson; L. S. "Tiny" Keen; M. V. Smith (Harry T. Pinson, with a broken leg, and Floyd K. "Buck" Buckner, with an injured leg, did not suit up for this game)
Centre College: Tanner; Herb Covington; Bartlett, Rubarth, Gibson, Bene, Lemon, Thomasson

ended in a scoreless tie. This was the first live football broadcast, via the campus ham radio station, whose call letters changed to 5YB in 1921 and was the forerunner of station WTAW, licensed in October 1922.

For the Dixie Classic, additional lines were opened between Dallas and Danville, to Louisville and Lexington, in Kentucky, and to Boston and Cambridge, in Massachusetts. The game reporting focused on the plays and seldom mentioned player names except at the coin toss and for those who scored a touchdown. The transmission for the Dixie Classic was relayed by a series of prearranged symbols keyed in Morse code, translated and read to the crowd on the receiving end, such as the following: "AM A 33 Y; AM P 8Y G; 2 D AM A 10 Y; TD AM P Wilson–EVANS." Decoded for the listeners, this meant, "Aggies' ball at the 33-yard line; Aggie pass, 8-yard gain; second down Aggies at 10-yard line; Aggie touchdown, pass Puny Wilson to A. J. Evans."[35]

Needless to say, January 2, 1922, was an exciting day in downtown Bryan. Crowds gathered early in the street in front of the Wallace Building in advance of the play-by-play relay of the big game from Dallas.[36]

KICKOFF

Coach Bible had done all he could to prepare his team. In spite of the thinned ranks, they had practiced hard, literally up until the last hours before going to Fair Park. Bible was a master of the pregame talk, and his calm speech was brief and to the point. No one knew that only moments before the game, Col. Ike Ashburn, a decorated veteran of the war and member of the NCAA nominating committee, informed Bible that he had been named as the first and only southern coach on the prestigious National Football Rules Committee, a position of high honor he would hold for the next three decades. Focused on preparing the Aggies, he softly spoke his final pregame words:[37]

> Gentlemen, I know you all realize and accept your responsibility on this occasion. You are not only representing Texas A&M College; you are representing the Southwest Conference, its schools, its teams, its alumni, and its friends. This afternoon you are facing perhaps the greatest football team in the nation. With all this in mind, how can you do less than turn in a winning effort?[38]

Puny Wilson, asked years later what Bible said prior to the game, replied, "I'm not sure. He spoke a few well-chosen words, and man, *we were ready!*"

Shortly after two-thirty, with the crowd standing and cheering, team captains Heine Weir and Red Roberts met at midfield. The Aggies won the coin toss and elected to receive and defend the west goal "with a fairly stiff wind blowing up the field at the pursuer's back." The field was dry, the perfect setting for the Colonels' swift-running offense. Red Roberts teed up the ball for the kickoff. Legend is that Bo McMillin told Red to "kick to the little guy on the left side." One of the smallest players on the field, Sammy Sanders received the high kick on the 9-yard line. Sanders recalls, "I was so scared I dropped the ball, yet once picked up and under way, the goal posts seemed to be racing toward me." The return covered 45 yards, past midfield, and the *Dallas Morning News* reporter noted, "The shifty-footed all-conference back eluded every Centre player except a lone defender between him and the goal line: Bo McMillin." With great field position at midfield, the Aggies quickly gained a first down, but they were abruptly stopped when captain and running back Heine Weir suffered a broken leg and was carried from the field.[39]

The loss of Weir was a critical event. During this era of college football, neither the coach nor any other team assistant was allowed to "coach from the sidelines," which included sending in plays. There were no coaches in the press box and no headset communication with the sidelines. These rules, enforced by a 15-yard penalty, were being relaxed in the early 1920s, but the

The dramatic picture at the Dixie Classic of the Aggie goal line defense holding the Prayin' Colonels after four attempts. The Aggies took over on the 6-inch line during the closing minutes of the first half. Note the striped uniforms. Jerseys with the single stripe on gray are the Aggies, and the number on the back of uniform jerseys was used for the first time in the fall of 1920. (Source: Cushing Memorial Library and Archives)

team captain on the field called the plays and formations on both offense and defense. In addition to there being no special teams or rotation of players in and out of the game, there were few time-outs. The overall strategy and game plan had been determined by Coach Bible before the game and was to be executed by Weir on the field. However, once the game started, Weir—and after his injury, his substitute, Wilson—made the on-the-field calls from a selection of ten to twelve plays. The numerous punts on first down deep in A&M's territory were predetermined as a tactic by Bible to reduce the likelihood of a fumble or interception close to the Aggie goal. Puny Wilson would later receive accolades for the way he stepped forward to call signals and lead the team following Weir's injury.[40]

Unable to move the ball, the Aggies saw their drive stalled. Punter Tom Miller booted the ball 60 yards, down to the goal line, where Centre fullback Tom Bartlett was standing. He caught the ball and, stepping back to run around the end to avoid the oncoming punt coverage, was immediately tackled 3 yards deep in the end zone for a safety by Aggie halfback Wilson, whose "speed cut [Bartlett] down before he could get over [the goal line]." Centre star halfback Red Roberts twisted his knee on the play but remained in the game. The impact of Red's injury on the outcome of the game would be debated for years, though, oddly enough, there was little attention paid to the loss of Heine Weir and four other Aggie players in the first half of the game. Many of the excited fans in the stands did not even realize what had happened on the goal line. Those at the game recall that even the referees seemed surprised when the Aggies put two points on the scoreboard within the first few minutes of play. This was the first time all season the Prayin' Colonels had trailed in a game.[41]

Following the touch-back (safety), Centre dominated the rest of the first half. There were three series when the Colonels had great field position and should have scored. After a Centre punt, Sammy Sanders caught the ball, juggled it, and the ball hit the ground. As he tried to pick it up he was hit by Centre defender Bill Shadoan, who was running full speed. Sanders was knocked totally unconscious, "the ball dropping from his nerveless fingers," and Shadoan pounced on the ball on the Aggie 28.

Three plunges gained 7 yards, then A&M was whistled for holding, and the 15-yard penalty resulted in the ball being placed on the Aggies' 6-yard line. It was first and goal. First Bo, then Snowday, then Army hit the stiffened Aggie line, and the ball rested on the 6-inch line. On fourth down and goal, Bo fumbled and recovered the snap, but the delay caused him to just get back the line of scrimmage. Texas A&M took over, mere inches from the goal line and, lined up in short punt formation, kicked it away on first down.

Centre took over at midfield. Bo, at quarterback, hit Covington, playing bareheaded, for 15, and the little speedster picked up another 10 yards, for a Centre first down on the 15. With great field position, Centre moved to the 9, but once again the Aggie defense held, Bo fumbled, and DuBois of A&M recovered on the 9-yard line.

Robertson noted, "It was the second time that it appeared the Colonels were going to put points on the board and they had nothing to show for their efforts. The offense that Uncle Charlie had installed depended on split-second timing and field position. He had his team run signal drills over and over, perfecting the precision of the offense. The lack of practice time on the long trip, and Bo having missed many of the sessions in Dallas, was beginning to show, as drive after drive stalled and the Colonels simply weren't sharp."[42]

After the Aggies' recovery of Bo's second fumble, they couldn't move the ball and had to punt again. Herb Covington returned the ball to the A&M 28-yard line: great field position again. Bo went to the air. Two passes were incomplete and the third picked up 5 yards. On the fourth straight aerial attempt, Bo threw the first interception of the day, his pass picked off by an Aggie defender. Following A&M's loss of Weir, Sanders, and Morris, who was knocked out of much of the second quarter, the half ended after a brief exchange of punts with the ball in A&M's possession near midfield and with A&M still having a "commanding" lead of 2–0.

Postgame reporting picked up nationwide was primarily a general overview of the match, with little emphasis or even mention of A&M injuries by either the Associated Press report or veteran Texas sportswriter Jinx Tucker, who wrote for the *Waco News-Tribune*.[43] However, the very best perspective on the condition and injuries on the A&M team by the end of the first half was presented by Dr. E. King Gill, in an article thirty-four years after the game. Gill was in the press box, spotting for Jinx Tucker. From this play-by-play vantage point, and with his knowledge of the players, he gave a stark account of the Aggie situation: "Our entire starting backfield and one backfield replacement went out in the first quarter: Sammy knocked out cold and later suffered a twisted knee; Heine Weir, captain, [with a] broken leg; Bull Johnson, fullback, lost, and we also lost quarterback A. B. 'Bugs' Morris and halfback Louis E. Miller."[44]

Bible, years later, was candid about the concerning situation: "With Weir [and the other players out], that 2–0 lead we owned at the end of the half seemed meaningless." If the Aggies could not field eleven players, they would have to forfeit the game. Concerned about being short of players, Bible looked up at the press box and waved for E. King Gill to come down to the field. "Suit up, boy," the coach said, "and be ready to play." Gill did suit up and stood ready to enter the game. (The full story of the famous Bible "wave" is covered in chapter 4.)

The staff of the *Bryan Daily Eagle,* an afternoon publication, with offices near where the game was being announced to the crowd in and around the Wallace Building, became so excited that they released their special daily issue at halftime (in what may have been a first) with the bold headline "First Half Aggies 2-to-0 over Centre." One may conjecture that the newspaper, not sure how the second half would unfold, was nervous concerning the final outcome of the game and eager to produce a positive headline for the home team.

The second half opened with Murrah of A&M kicking to Centre's leading game rusher, Covington, followed by a punting duel as each team fought for field position with the hope that the other would allow a turnover and an opportunity to score. Bible's account of the half is the best among many accounts:

> We had two great chances to score at the start of the second half. We fumbled both of them as Centre stopped us twice within the shadow of the goal line. They kicked out of danger but the punt was fumbled and Tanner recovered for Centre. Shortly afterward, the vaunted Colonel power showed itself. [Terry] Snoddy bucked over for the game's first touchdown and Red Roberts converted: 7–2—our margin vanished. The expected rout of the Aggies seemed underway.
>
> After Centre's first touchdown, Centre fumbled and left guard Cap Murrah recovered the ball at the Centre thirty-five, followed by Puny Wilson throwing a TD to Jack Evans, making the score 9–7. Everyone waited for the Kentucky avalanche, but once again it was the Texas Aggies that struck with lighting speed on the fleet feet of Puny Wilson. Behind perfect "interference" [blocking], Wilson broke free and raced 30 yards off-tackle around the right end to

score before the third period was over. McMillan's kick made it 16–7 and for the first time in the game, an upset loomed.

It was a desperate, overanxious Centre team that started the fourth quarter in an effort to overtake the Aggies. Desperation, however, can produce disastrous results. Bo McMillin, who never quite lived up to his All-American rating in the game, was hampered by a bad pass from Centre early in the period. He got off a wobbly pass that landed in the arms of the Aggies' Ted Winn (left tackle when on offense, and linebacker on defense). Winn scored and, though Bill McMillan failed to convert, the 15-point margin seemed big enough.

Bible concluded, "With 10 minutes remaining, the Colonels tried every trick in the book. Finally, in the waning minutes, a tricky forward-lateral maneuver on which McMillin passed to Covington, who then lateraled to Snoddy, gave them their second touchdown. Roberts kicked the extra point, but that in itself was a futile gesture. The mighty Prayin' Colonels of Centre were beaten."[45]

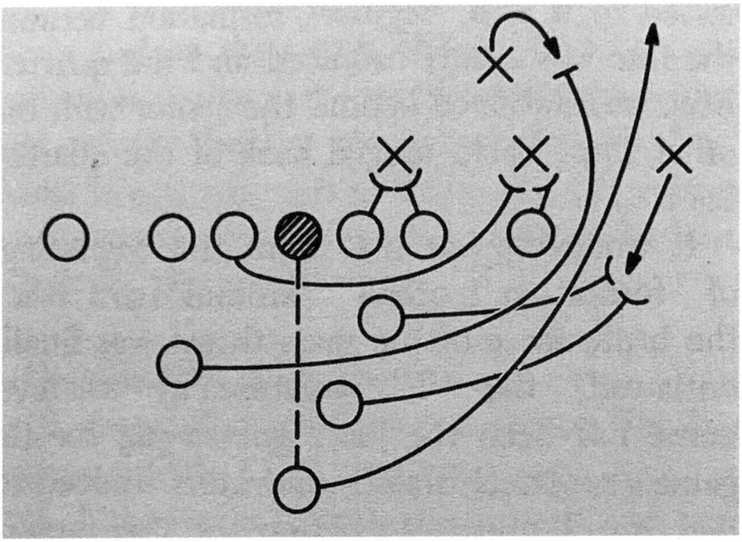

Bible's off-tackle play from what was called a "short punt formation." In the third quarter the play set up successful drives and scored the winning touchdown. The play included a direct snap to the fullback with the left halfback leading the play around the right side. (Source: Adapted from Kern Tips, Football—Texas Style*)*

Texas A&M	2	0	14	6	—22
Centre College	0	0	7	7	—14

A&M	Safety Puny Wilson tackled Bartlett in end zone, 2
Centre	Snoddy, 3-yard run, Roberts kick, 7
A&M	A. J. Evans, 15-yard pass from Puny Wilson, McMillan kick, 7
A&M	Puny Wilson, 30-yard run, McMillan kick, 7
A&M	Ted Winn, 45-yard interception for TD, kick failed, 6
Centre	Covington, 2-yard pass from Bo McMillin, Roberts kick, 7

The Aggies never had a sustained drive, punted a dozen times, and had only five first downs, compared to fourteen for the Colonels. Bo McMillin, playing in his last collegiate game, completed only three passes. The leading rusher of the game was the Colonels' substitute Herb Covington, with 137 yards on twenty-two carries, out of a total of 314 yards gained by Centre. At the end of the game, as fans swarmed the field, the Colonels stood in midfield and cheered, "Hip, Hip, Hooray for the Aggies! Hip, Hip, Hooray for the Aggies!"[46]

The intense year-end preparation with a select squad of cadets had led to success. Bible was very proud of his disciplined team. Of Bible's comments, the *Eagle* would later report, "The unassuming genius of Aggie play for the last four years, regarded by players and officials as the real reason of the victory, gives all credit to his men," with Bible telling the AP sports reporter in a "special" release nationwide, "The A. and M. players were attuned to the proper attitude and they won. The men went in with the spirit of self-sacrifice, giving up the enjoyments of Christmas week to put themselves in proper physical condition. They were imbued with the fighting spirit the Aggies have always shown. They did it. They played a splendid game."[47]

East Coast football enthusiasts and sports writers awoke to a story in the *New York Times* reporting on the Dixie Classic: "The Texans presented a defense that was well-nigh impregnable, while on the offense they uncovered a series of tricky and versatile attacks that had Centre men completely at sea." A cartoon, titled simply "Taps!," followed in the *Boston Post,* summarizing the Colonels' defeat at the hands of the Aggies, while back in College Station the local *Eagle* boasted, "They fought every inch of the way—they played rings around the famed team and rose to the supreme height of the glory of the old Aggie spirit that has immortalized College Station teams." The 1922 *Longhorn,* dedicated to Coach Bible, concluded: "As far as fighting is concerned, the Center [*sic*] fray is a second [Texas] Longhorn battle. Both will go down in gridiron history as a fitting climax to the season in which the Farmers fought all the harder as things looked the darkest and in which, through their persistence, they eventually made one of the most brilliant records that any A. & M. team has ever made."[48]

And yet, despite such emphasis on "Aggie spirit," there were no media reports immediately following the game about E. King Gill suiting up, including the January 3 article filed by Jinx Tucker, who sat next to Gill the entire first half in the press box and was aware of his departure to the field.

AGGIE BRAND OF FOOTBALL

Outweighed, suffering numerous game injuries, and heavily favored to lose to the powerhouse Colonels, the Aggies notched one of the most important victories in college football history. Indeed, the win had significant implications beyond Aggie football and elation over the outcome. Texas teams had for over a decade fielded very competitive teams, yet outside the Southwest they received little or no attention. The only team across the greater South that received routine mention in the eastern sports media was Georgia Tech, and even then, the "Ramblin' Wreck" only obtained limited coverage. The *Texas Aggie* alumni newspaper was thrilled to hail the win and place the victory in context of the feat accomplished: "It was a surprise, but in no way can the victory be called a fluke. The 11,554 spectators at the new stadium saw native sons run roughshod over the Southern Champions, saw them outplay and out-general the conquerors of Harvard, Auburn, Tulane, Arizona, and Washington and Lee, and were amazed at the wonderful exhibition of football from a team which had not been given an outside chance to win."[49]

Among the very credible sources that vaulted the Aggies and Southwest football into national recognition were the three officials who called the Dixie Classic. The formation of the NCAA and the SWC had mandated neutral-expert officiating. The added benefit, in the case of the A&M–Centre game, was that all three officials were well-recognized experts on football. Most importantly, they were allowed open access to the sports media to give their assessment of games once they were completed. The three officials for the Classic were referee Ernie Quigley, umpire Robert W. "Tiny" Maxwell, and head linesman R. D. Sproul.[50]

At ground level in the trenches with the two teams during that afternoon in Dallas, the trio provided some of the most detailed and perceptive assessments of the game. Quigley expressed that "the Aggies' victory stamped the brand of football played in the Southwest as equal to that offered anywhere. A&M played on its toes during the entire contest. The 'breaks' went to the Aggies, because they were on deck to take them. Coach Bible is due a great deal of credit for his work in developing the A&M team to such a high point."[51]

The reporting from Dallas ruffled the feathers of the Eastern establishment football powers, including Harvard, Yale, and Princeton, who felt they had a corner on college football and that they should dominate the news and any other outside teams. After Tiny Maxwell (for whom the Maxwell Trophy is named), in his postgame column in the *Philadelphia Evening Public Ledger,* concluded, "The Aggies would have beaten any team in the country barring none; the team played unbeatable football. I cannot give too much praise to Coach Bible and the members of the team . . . football critics and fans over the nation cannot but recognize in them one of the greatest teams ever assembled." Harvard was the first to cry foul that the game in Dallas did not deserve such attention and praise. However, Maxwell, having refereed Centre's stunning victory over Harvard in Cambridge earlier in the 1921 season, was in a unique position to draw his conclusions.[52]

THE FORGOTTEN ALL-AMERICANS

Maxwell and Quigley further opened up the discussion, along with Jinx Tucker of the *Waco News-Tribune,* over who were the annual outstanding college players and who should be selected as All-Americans. Maxwell strongly noted that A&M's Cap Murrah was "the greatest lineman I have seen in five years." Quigley followed up with comments at the banquet honoring the victorious Aggies, and his remarks were published in the papers: "If there was to be another all-American team selected, I would head it with Puny Wilson, and right behind him come Cap Murrah (as well as Jack Evans and Tom Miller)." Though college football in the South had been ignored historically, Jinx Tucker concluded that "the Aggie victory shocked football fans" nationwide and would forever change the annual selection of the All-American team. Joe Utay, southwestern writer for the national publication *Spalding's Official Intercollegiate Foot Ball Guide,* wrote, "It was a brilliant game from beginning to end and ranks among the most exciting games ever played in the Southwest. This game should give the Southwest its proper recognition in the East. The team had a number of star players. Murrah was the best lineman in the Southwest; he is a big, powerful and aggressive guard. Sanders, Carruthers, Morris, Buckner, Evans, and Miller are other players who deserve special mention."[53]

The *Battalion* zeroed in on the All-American selection process: "We threw a wrench late in the cogs of the machine which picks the mystical All-American team when we downed Centre College to the surprise of everyone except ourselves." One key indicator is that Walter Camp, who was at the Rose Bowl to watch a 0–0 tie, had, for two decades prior to 1922, controlled the selection of the annual national All-American honorees, a process dominated by an eastern bias for Ivy League players that disregarded players from the South and West. During this period only four southern players had been named to the prestigious list, and three of them played in the Dixie Classic. Texas colleges and sports fans had good reason to be irritated with the All-American process and national rankings.

During this time of national obsession with college football, Walter Camp and the East Coast football establishment and media had all but ignored football in the South and Southwest in general and the state of Texas in particular. In addition to Texas A&M's four tremendous winning seasons from 1917 to 1921, in which they lost only three games, championship teams and prospective—yet forgotten—All-Americans included the Texas Longhorns, with three undefeated seasons in 1914, 1918, and 1920. University of Texas players Clyde Littlefield, Ray Keck, Gustav "Pig" Ditmar, and K. L. Berry were outstanding, yet unrecognized nationally. Similarly, SMU was 9–0 in 1923, including star players Gene Bedford and Logan Stollenwerck. Likewise, Herman Clark, Raymond "Rags" Matthews, and their teammates at TCU were 9–1 in 1920, coached by former A&M coach William L. Driver; and Baylor, with star running back Rusty Blailock, won the SWC title in 1915 with a 7–1 record, following with a winning record in both 1916 (9–1) and 1922.[54]

But after the Aggies' dramatic victory in the 1922 Dixie Classic, permanent changes would come in the attention and respect given college football in the South and Southwest.[55]

CHAPTER 4

The 12th Man

Enthusiasm, pride, loyalty—these are traits to be found in almost any successful college program. But when these qualities become a religion, as they have at Texas A&M, they create a rather miraculous atmosphere which can be best described as "The Twelfth Man" spirit. It is a spirit which has worked not only on football fields across the nation, but on battlefields throughout the world.

—Wilbur Evans and H. B. McElroy '38, *The Twelfth Man: A Story of Texas A&M Football* (1974)

The most spectacular, most nerve tingling football game ever staged in the history of the game in the Southwest.

—*Bryan Eagle*, January 3, 1922

The story and analysis of the victory of the Fightin' Texas Aggies over national powerhouse Centre College in January 1922 dominated the sports pages across the nation for weeks and focused attention on football in the South and Southwest—a focus that continues to this day. The grit needed by the Aggies to remain in the game after a number of serious injuries to the team's starters, along with Coach Dana Bible's insistence on a strong and aggressive defense, won the day. I have long wondered if the sportswriters in the Fair Park press box and the fans behind the A&M bench noticed either the mounting injuries by the end of the first half or the presence of E. King Gill, the lone player standing near the coach in the third quarter. What they may have failed to notice at the time was not lost on Bible and the team. The actions of Coach Bible and King Gill that day have transcended those moments on the sidelines at the Dixie Classic and evolved into a cherished Aggie tradition steeped in legend and lore.

Hundreds of accounts of the Aggie 12th Man tradition have been written, some broadcast on radio or TV and all repeated many times, about those moments in Dallas on the afternoon of January 2, 1922, when Gill

E. King Gill. (Source: Cushing Memorial Library and Archives)

descended from the press box to suit up in an injured player's uniform for the Aggie team. As time and legend have passed through the generations it has become one of the bedrock traditions of Texas A&M, surpassed only by Silver Taps and Aggie Muster, held annually on April 21. Indeed, the legend has grown and evolved over the years. In addition to my several chats with Dr. Gill about the events of that day and my conversations with Joe Utay '08, who conceived and promoted the first Dixie Classic game, there are three parallel primary accounts of the Dixie Classic given by Gill and Bible that form the basis of this presentation. The three sources include an audio interview with D. X. Bible conducted by Dr. Tom Harrington in 1969; a detailed article in the January 19, 1956, *Houston Post,* "A&M's First Twelfth Man"; and the original draft and notes in the margin of E. King Gill's 1964 campus Muster speech, delivered on the steps of the Texas A&M System Administration Building. Cushing Archives has preserved remarkable audio files of the live Muster presentation by Gill, including his introduction by President James Earl Rudder '32.[1]

King Gill, a sophomore cadet in the fall of 1921, had opted, with the approval of the coaches, not to continue on the football team in order to concentrate on a starting position on the A&M basketball team. On New Year's Eve Gill had returned to his home in Dallas for a visit and to attend the football game. Lacking the $3 needed to pay admission, he joined the team at the stadium in order to get in, and he remained on the sidelines during pregame warm-ups. Coach Bible was aware that Waco sportswriter Jinx Tucker had asked Gill to join him in the press box to help spot the Aggie players. The hard-fought first half ended with the Aggies holding a slim 2-point lead, their ranks depleted due to injuries.

THE WAVE

Dr. King Gill recalled in 1956:

> It was at that point that I glanced down at our bench. Old D.X. was waving at the press box and motioning toward the empty bench. He knew I was up there. He had seen me leave with Jinx. And I knew what he wanted.
>
> I ran down through the bleachers and jumped onto the field. I'll never forget what he said to me: "Boy," he said, "it doesn't look like I'm going to have enough players to finish the game. You may have to go in there and stand around for a while."
>
> That was all there was to it. The next thing I knew, they hustled me under the grandstand. They didn't have dressing rooms in those days. They handed me Heine Weir's uniform and told me to get into it. I got into it, all right, as fast I could.[2]

There are reports that the Aggie yell leaders helped get King down from the press box and ready to play.

Prior to the game Coach Bible was reported to have traveled to Dallas with only eighteen players (not including Gill) from his season-ending roster of thirty-five. The official pregame program listed twenty-four A&M players, and E. King Gill was listed as an active player, which was very misleading. The unidentified image of him sitting in the middle of the team picture beside team captain Heine Weir (and the other team members who did not suit up) appeared in the picture taken in October 1921. This promotional picture was submitted by the A&M press office for the Dixie Classic final program before Gill opted out in order to play basketball and before Bible selected his traveling squad for Dallas. Two days before the game, after an injury to running back Buck Buckner in practice that relegated him to crutches on the sidelines, the Aggies were left with a total of seventeen healthy players at the start of the game. By the end of the first half, the bench was cleared, with Bill McMillan, assisted by Puny Wilson, replacing Bugs Morris at quarterback. After Weir broke his leg and Sammy Sanders was knocked out, Tiny Keen and Ben Beesley rotated in the backfield and also played linebacker on defense, along with Tuffy Wendt. M. V. Smith subbed at end for both Wilson and Jack Evans. At the start of the second half of play there were only eleven Aggies on the field to play both ways—offense and defense—and no available substitutes. If they dropped below eleven players on the field, they would have to forfeit the game.[3]

Thus, King Gill stepped from below the bleachers, onto the sidelines, and into the annals of Aggie history and lore. Little did he, or any others at that moment, realize that the tradition of the 12th Man had been born. Nevertheless, over the years it would grow to symbolize selfless service and the spirit of the Fightin' Texas Aggies.

King Gill recalled that after he suited up:

> All of our boys managed to survive from that point forward. And they even went on to win the game. That is the story, exactly as it happened. I wish I could say I ran for the winning touchdown. But I didn't. I simply got ready and waited, just in case I was needed.

In the years after the Dixie Classic, Gill was asked numerous times how the 12th Man tradition finally took hold with the Aggies. It took the tradition more than a decade to come into its own. Gill explained:

> I really couldn't say for sure how it caught hold. There was, of course, some talk about the incident immediately after the game. I think it was mentioned in a few newspapers. But there wasn't a whole lot said.

> I really didn't hear much about it until 15 years later. It caught hold, I think, at the time A. &. M. football teams were at the top of the heap—when John Kimbrough ['39] and those boys were in school. By that time, of course, the cadet corps had begun the practice of standing at football games.[4]

REMEMBER THE ALAMO

The Aggies were able to prevail in Dallas with the final eleven players on the field, and King Gill did not play that day in the Dixie Classic. However, few are aware that this star athlete won seven letters at Texas A&M: in football, in basketball (as an all-conference center), and in baseball (as a pitcher). Also, in the same year as the Dixie Classic, he played on the 1922 Aggie football team that beat Texas on Thanksgiving. Gill's greatest on-the-field moment included scoring a 25-yard touchdown at old Clark Field in Austin followed by a long run from scrimmage to the Texas 4-yard line, setting up a second winning score. Players recalled Coach Bible's masterful halftime talk at that game, which emulated the often-reported legend by Colonel William B. Travis, commander at the Alamo in March 1836. Bible drew an imaginary line across the floor and said, "Those who want to go out and be known as members of an A&M team that defeated Texas in Austin, step across this line." Bible narrated the incident to sportswriter Kern Tips, who reported, "He was almost knocked down by the unanimous rush!" A&M went on to win, 14–7.[5]

On returning to campus, King Gill was introduced briefly by yell leader Harry W. "Red" Thompson '21 as "the 12th Man" during a yell practice on the steps of the YMCA, but scant attention was paid and there was no mention in the 1922 *Longhorn* yearbook of the event. There was, however, a grand victory celebration for the team and cadets in Sbisa Dining Hall. The cooks at the mess hall worked nonstop for eight hours to prepare a huge cake seven feet long and layered in a pyramid more than three feet high. The 340-pound dessert had 40 pounds of jelly between the layers and 50 pounds of maroon and white icing. On the top of the cake was a replica of a football, and along the side of the cake was inscribed: "Greetings Farmers, Welcome, 100%, A&M, Jan 2, 1922." The score of 22–14 was displayed on little candy footballs. After a round of speeches, each player was given a small gold football engraved with a "T" and embedded with a diamond. When the surprise cake was rolled out, it was met with loud whooping and cheers by the cadets, staff, and faculty, followed by over a thousand slices served to the crowd.[6]

Over the next two decades, as King Gill noted, there would be scant reference to the 12th Man event and tradition. During the early and mid-1920s there were a number of references to the "twelfth man," but no mention of King Gill. Interestingly, the moniker was used in the *Battalion* in editorials on the reaction to competition around the conference, primarily in a growing rift between A&M and Baylor, when in October 1923, the paper reported "the entire student body elected itself the twelfth man on the team."[7] The full meaning of the "twelfth man" was expressed in the days before the Thanksgiving rivalry with Texas in 1924, in an editorial titled, "To the Corps":

> Your task in the annual classic of the Southwest is of huge proportions. *You are the twelfth man on that team,* and the outcome of the game depends upon you. Your attitude and feelings will be reflected in the team out on the field by some unexplainable process of transmittance. As you fight [and yell], so will those eleven maroon-jersied warriors fight. Fight hard, fight Aggies![8]

The Aggies returned a number of times to Dallas to play at Fair Park, particularly against another upstart small-college team, the Suwannee Tigers of Tennessee, with Bible's team going 4 and 0. One writer noted, "It is hard to beat 12 men on the football field, especially when that twelfth man is the famous Aggie cadet corps."[9]

An aerial shot was taken of a 12th Man formation spelled out at halftime by band and cadet corps on Kyle Field in the early 1930s. The 12th Man spirit was used by Coach Matty Bell in 1930 when he called on the cadets to provide a center and Joe Love '33 stepped forward (he would letter in 1931 and 1932). The tradition seemed to gain momentum as the Aggies prepared to go to Fort Worth in the fall of 1933. One observer noted, "They're making plans to bury the T.C.U. 'jinx' as they follow the team—that's among the khaki-clad cadets who make up the football team's famous '12th Man,' however, and among the thousands of former students over the countryside."[10]

"GILL PUT AGGIES ON THEIR FEET"

However, the tradition did not get wide attention until the Aggies' run for the national championship in 1939–40. Arrangements for the Sugar Bowl game were handled by Dean Edwin Kyle, who coordinated extensive media coverage for Texas A&M with an advertising blitz on more than three hundred radio stations on the NBC Blue network. For pregame publicity, E. E. McQuillen '20, Association of Former Students executive director (known by many as "Mr. Mac"), was asked to come up with an Aggie sports story for the "Pigskin Parade" segment of *The Kraft Music Hall* radio program (which would be followed by Bing Crosby's hour of the show), to be broadcast prior to the Sugar Bowl on WSM in Nashville. McQuillen came up with a series of segments that included the Aggie Band, the Singing Cadets, yell leaders, and the story of the 12th Man. McQuillen's connection with the past—a former all-conference basketball star, he had firsthand knowledge of the events in Dallas and had been King Gill's basketball coach in 1921–23—allowed him to chronicle the story of the events in Dallas at the Dixie Classic twenty years prior, with WSM broadcasting a dramatization of the 1922 A&M–Centre game. McQuillen, a former all-conference basketball star, had first-hand knowledge of the events in Dallas and had been King Gill's basketball coach in 1921–23. With all the excitement over football, few recall that the Aggies produced four outright SWC basketball championships between 1920 and 1923. King Gill agreed that the pregame programming before the Sugar Bowl marked the moment when the 12th Man tradition gained its first wide awareness. McQuillen's story captured the imagination of the listeners and was broadcast several times, becoming ingrained in Aggie lore in the process.[11]

McQuillen would also have a pivotal role in reporting and crafting the significance of the Aggie Muster tradition, which had its major start after Aggie troops on Corregidor in April 1942, despite being in the heat of battle, managed to carry on the Aggie San Jacinto tradition. Today the Texas Aggie Muster tradition is observed at hundreds of locations worldwide each April. Interestingly, King Gill was stationed in the Philippines as a medical officer shortly after the Japanese were driven out, and he made a trip across Manila Bay to visit Corregidor, the site of the '42 Muster and the revered tradition it originated. Gill recalled that the troops had hardly landed and unpacked when a note appeared on the unit bulletin board that there would be a meeting of all the Texas Aggies. One of the other doctors in the unit, not an Aggie, quipped, "You damn Aggies have just landed and you are already holding meetings." Of course, it wasn't just any meeting; it was Aggie Muster. Dozens of Aggies had converged on Manila from all over the Philippines, meeting at the corner bar and lobby at the Manila Hotel to plan the trip to "the Rock." Robert A. "Bob" Epstein '44 recalled, "In Manila, starting a couple of days before Muster, like on a Corps trip, Aggies began to assemble. They gathered corps-trip style in the lobby of the Manila Hotel and greeted old friends. Aggies were lounging around everywhere and engaged in good old Aggie bull sessions. We didn't get much sleep and we didn't march into town. But we took three crash boats to Corregidor; it was all intimately familiar, just like the corps trip routine."[12]

KIDDIE KORPS

Coach Homer Norton again invoked the 12th Man when the team needed a center in 1941, and nine cadets came forward to fill the position. In the same year, Lillian Munnerlyn, wife of A&M poultry science professor Ford Munnerlyn '26, penned the words and music to the song "The Twelfth Man." The new song was introduced to the cadets on September 23, 1941, at the Tuesday night yell practice on the steps of Goodwin Hall in advance of the annual bonfire. This became only the third fight song accepted by the cadets.[13]

The 12th Man
Texas Aggies down in Aggieland
We've got Aggie Spirit to a man!
Stand united! That's the Aggie theme.
We're the twelfth man on the team,
When we're down, the goin's rough and tough
We just grin and yell; we've got the stuff
To fight together for the Aggie dream
We're the twelfth man on that
FIGHTIN' AGGIE TEAM

The story of the 1922 Dixie Classic and A&M's victory was told and retold. It was featured on the New Year's Day *Southern Select Sports* program on KPRC in Houston in 1943, followed by a feature story in the *Houston Post*. The spirit of the 12th Man was alive and well as Coach Homer Norton, during the depths of World War II, called on the cadets to walk on and fill the 1943 team roster. In addition to taking nearly the entire coaching staff, enlistment in the military and the draft had, by mid-1943, taken most able-bodied players who were eighteen or older. A host of sixteen- and seventeen-year-olds on campus came forward with little experience but a lot of heart to fill what became known as the "Kiddie Korps" or "Whiz Kids" team. Regardless of the fact that the Aggie lineup changed every week, the team posted a surprising 7–2–1 record. To spur morale, acting A&M President Frank Bolton, upon the recommendation of Dean Kyle, agreed to approve a postseason invitation to the Orange Bowl. And in spite of tight wartime travel restrictions, the Aggies were able to secure special train travel to Miami. Cramped in regular commuter passenger cars, the team slept sitting up for two nights, had no exercise, and missed regular meals. Houston sportswriter Mickey Herskowitz noted, "Coach Norton believed they left their game on the train," because they lost to LSU, 19–14. Soon after the bowl game the *Austin Statesman* had one of the earliest articles about King Gill and the 12th Man under the headline "Gill Put Aggies on Their Feet," noting, "Colonel Gill [called to active duty], reputedly the man responsible for the tradition that keeps Texas A&M cadets on their feet throughout every football game, now is a flight surgeon" in the Army Air Corps serving in the Philippines.[14]

The graduating A&M class of 1980 funded a life-size bronze statue of King Gill, sculpted by Houston artist George Foley, that stands at the north end of Kyle Field. The Aggie student body was further linked to the 12th Man when a banner with four-foot-high letters was unfurled on the second deck of Kyle Field during the November 2, 1968, A&M–Arkansas game. The banner carried the words "The Twelfth Man Is Here." In time this was shortened to the slogan "Home of the 12th Man," with permanent letters affixed on the student side and dedicated on September 17, 1988, following a gift of $10,000 from the Class of 1988. On the west side of Kyle Field occupied by the alumni, letters were added that read: "Welcome to Aggieland."[15]

NO PRIOR EXPERIENCE REQUIRED

In the fall of 1982, football head coach Jackie Sherrill participated in construction of the annual Thanksgiving Bonfire and was very impressed with the esprit de corps and determination of the students in advance of the Texas game. Shortly after that the coach spoke to the cadets in Duncan Dining Hall at the evening meal and invited them to walk on and be a part of a new 12th Man kickoff squad. Word spread fast, and others outside the Corps wanted to participate. Cadet Corps Commander Mike Holmes recalled, "It's like letting us be the original 12th Man," which was presumably

The 12th Man statue of E. King Gill at Texas A&M. (Source: Cushing Memorial Library and Archives)

exactly the response Coach Sherrill had in mind. A now-famous advertisement was placed in the *Battalion:*

> Persons interested in trying out for the Twelfth Man Kickoff Team need to report to Kyle Field Dressing Room on Monday, Feb. 21, at 5 p.m. No prior experience required.[16]

More than 250 students showed up to try out for the ten available positions on the squad. The action created nationwide publicity and spread the story and tradition of the Aggie 12th Man from coast to coast. Former Aggie quarterback and graduate assistant David Beal '81 was tasked with trimming the pool prior to the opening of fall practice, with the result that thirty-six walk-ons were invited to practice; by late August, seventeen students had been selected. The kickoff squad would only participate in home games. The unit took the field for the first time against the California Golden Bears at Kyle Field on September 3, 1983. The first 12th Man tackle was made by senior Ike Liles of Stamford, Texas, assisted by Tom Christner and Leroy Hallman. Over the next five seasons the original 12th Man unit held opponents to an average of 12.5 yards per return. In 1991 head coach R. C. Slocum reduced the squad to a single walk-on player wearing number 12.[17]

In the fall of 1985 the 12th Man towels, also originated by Jackie Sherrill, became a major part of game tradition when first waved by the 12th Man kickoff teams. The idea for the towel came from Pittsburgh and has been used by numerous teams. The Aggie 12th Man towels soon became a well-accepted, nearly ubiquitous item among fans. One exciting incident occurred during the 1988 Cotton Bowl Classic against Notre Dame, when a member of the 12th Man kickoff team, Warren Barhorst '88, tackled Heisman Trophy winner Tim Brown, snatched the "ND" towel from his belt, and waved it over his head in celebration. An infuriated Brown pursued and tackled Barhorst—and was flagged for a 15-yard penalty for unsportsmanlike conduct. The Aggies, following a third straight SWC championship, hosted the Cotton Bowl and won the game 35–10 before a crowd of over seventy-three thousand.

The "12th Man" term and usage have been copied by a number of professional football teams and other organizations, even though at the time the moniker and claim were over 80 years old. The term "12th Man" is licensed to Texas A&M, with patent number 1948306 issued by the US Patent and Trademark Office in Washington in September 1990. In 2005 the

A 12th Man team on the sidelines, 1980s. (Source: Courtesy Aggieland *yearbook)*

Chicago Bears and the Buffalo Bills organizations agreed not to use the phrase, yet the Seattle Seahawks objected. A January 2006 suit filed by Texas A&M against Seattle to protect the 12th Man trademark was settled out of court in May 2006. The agreement licensed the trademark to

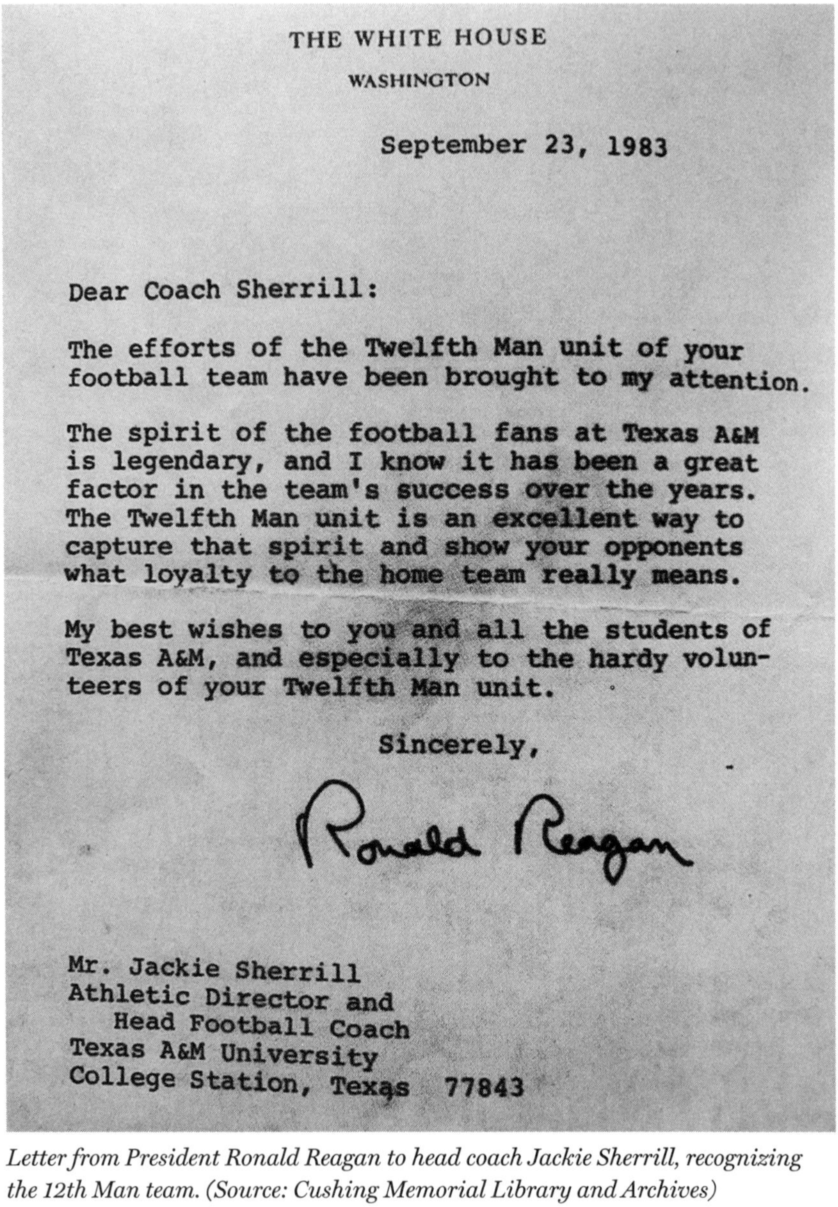

THE WHITE HOUSE

WASHINGTON

September 23, 1983

Dear Coach Sherrill:

The efforts of the Twelfth Man unit of your football team have been brought to my attention.

The spirit of the football fans at Texas A&M is legendary, and I know it has been a great factor in the team's success over the years. The Twelfth Man unit is an excellent way to capture that spirit and show your opponents what loyalty to the home team really means.

My best wishes to you and all the students of Texas A&M, and especially to the hardy volunteers of your Twelfth Man unit.

Sincerely,

Ronald Reagan

Mr. Jackie Sherrill
Athletic Director and
Head Football Coach
Texas A&M University
College Station, Texas 77843

Letter from President Ronald Reagan to head coach Jackie Sherrill, recognizing the 12th Man team. (Source: Cushing Memorial Library and Archives) the Seahawks in exchange for annual compensation along with a clear public acknowledgment by this NFL team that the ownership rested with Texas A&M.[18]

Bill Page '76, a keen observer of campus trends for over four decades, noted, "Over time, the ideal of the 12th Man has taken on a broader symbolism at Texas A&M. It has been incorporated into such diverse aspects of campus life as the name of a bus route to being adopted as the 'Twelfth Can'—the Aggie food bank program." And all of this is rooted in a time-honored tradition that began at the 1922 Dixie Classic in Dallas.

> *I wish I could say that I went in and ran for the winning touchdown. But I did not. I simply stood by in case my team needed me.*
>
> —E. King Gill

CHAPTER 5

Postscript

I've never seen a team as ready to play as A&M. The Aggies victory stamped the brand of football played in the Southwest as equal to that offered anywhere.

—Referee Ernie Quigley, January 3, 1922

There are certain qualities that a football coach must have to be successful. He must not only be versed in the technique of the game, but he must be a natural leader. No matter how able he may be as a strategist, no matter how thorough his knowledge of the fine points of the game may be, no matter how efficient he may be as a teacher, if he is not a leader who can inspire his men he does not belong in the coaching profession.

—Dana X. Bible, *Championship Football*

As with the inception of the famed 12th Man tradition at Texas A&M, the January 2, 1922, Dixie Classic generated years of postgame legacies, legends, and lore. The hype over the game, and its players, coaches, and fans, formed a pivotal moment for placing collegiate football in the South in the mainstream of national awareness and media coverage. Those involved with the Classic would influence an entire generation of athletes and fans of both college and the professional leagues as well as impact professional careers and accomplishments away from the gridiron. The game yielded greater recognition of football in the South, leading to a stream of players recognized as All-Americans, coaches sitting on NCAA rules committees, and national championships in 1935 and 1939. This final chapter seeks to highlight those who contributed to the lore of this golden age of football.

Uncle Charlie Moran remained at Centre College for the 1923 football season. The success of the little college competing with the big universities became the focus of detractors, including a disingenuous attack by the Southern Association of Colleges (SAC) at their annual meeting in Richmond. The association declared that Centre was overpaying their coach.

Dr. R. Ames Montgomery, Centre College president, incredulous at the suggestion, pointed out to the committee that Vanderbilt, Tulane, Washington and Lee, and South Carolina paid their coaches an average of $15,000; Coach Moran had received only $5,500 during the previous season and was considered liable to being hired away by the University of Alabama, which offered him $9,000.

The next attack at the usually mundane gathering included a resolution to decertify Centre College because it appeared they put "a disproportionate" emphasis on football. Again President Montgomery aggressively defended Centre.

It is interesting to consider the apparently close interest in Centre College's athletic achievements by administrators of other, competing schools. The timing of the initiatives mentioned above may also be suggestive, as Centre's enrollment was growing, the school was receiving national attention, and a new football stadium was opening. Any of these could be seen as a reason for jealousy among competitors, perhaps especially the University of Kentucky.

Meanwhile, Moran, the architect of Centre's fame and victories and the impetus for its new stadium, increased alumni giving, and new facilities, soon realized this was a very similar strategy to that used by Texas when he was beating them while coaching at Texas AMC. The other schools in Centre's conference, it seems, wanted Moran forced out, much as had been the case with the University of Texas–inspired witch-hunt in 1912. Robertson, in *The Wonder Team,* captured the essence of the attack: "Centre had literally owned the University of Kentucky since Uncle Charlie arrived at Centre. His record against the Wildcats was 6–0, and his teams had outscored UK by an incredible 200–3. In 24 quarters, 360 minutes of football, Kentucky had managed exactly one field goal!"[1]

Just like the cadets at Texas A&M years earlier, the students, staff, and alumni at Centre College were shocked by Uncle Charlie's low-key announcement that he was leaving to coach at Bucknell. After a limited search for a coach, Chief Myers stepped forward to coach the Prayin' Colonels, who once again beat Kentucky in 1924, 7–0.

After coaching at Bucknell (1924–26), Moran went on to coach for the NFL's Frankford Yellow Jackets (1927) and finally at Catawba College (1930–33). His overall college coaching record was 122–33–12. As previously mentioned, during the football off-season he served as a National League umpire for two decades, which including officiating four World Series, in 1927, 1929, 1933, and 1938. Centre's 6–0 upset victory over Harvard, commonly abbreviated at Centre College as "C6–H0" (even today campus buildings have telltale signs of the painted slogan), is cited as Moran's greatest win and is ranked by ESPN as the second-biggest upset in college football history. Coach Moran was proud of his small college team at Centre, noting years later, "I think the relationship established between Centre and Harvard paved the way for later friendly associations between the South and the North in football." Of course, the loss to Texas A&M in the Dixie Classic was a bitter defeat at the end of four great seasons at Centre.[2]

Coach Moran's earlier success at Texas A&M was never forgotten, as he was recognized in 1938 with "Charlie Moran Day." At the 1949 Thanksgiving game the members of the 1909–10 team were invited to College Station for ceremonies to honor the coach, but the reunion was marred by the coach's death a few months earlier. Uncle Charlie was honored with a plaque in the tunnel of the north end of Kyle Field. In 1968 he was named to the Texas A&M Athletic Hall of Fame.[3]

> To the Memory
> of
> CHARLES B. MORAN
> Great Coach
> of
> The Texas Aggies
> 1909–1914
>
> His indomitable spirit and inspiring
> leadership are enshrined forever
> in the records of the teams which
> he produced and in the hearts of
> the Aggies who played for him.
>
> "I DIDN'T COME HERE TO LOSE"[4]

Dana X. Bible, Moran's replacement, remained at Texas A&M until late 1928 and built the Southwest Conference's first traditional football power. Few are aware of the fact that after the departure of Uncle Charlie from Centre, Coach Bible was secretly offered the head coaching job for the Prayin' Colonels in 1924. He responded to Centre College:

> Many thanks for your telegram and I sincerely appreciate your interest but will be impossible to accept proposition at Centre. I am

> under contract here [Texas A&M] and very happily situated. Warm Personal Regards. D. X. Bible[5]

When his contract expired, he departed Texas A&M in 1928, upon the recommendation of Knute Rockne, and joined the Nebraska Cornhuskers, winning six conference championships in eight seasons in Lincoln. His success attracted the interest of the Texas Longhorns, who hired him in 1936 at a salary of $12,000. While in Austin he developed a plan to enhance recruitment of potential players. He established a network of prominent UT alumni around the state to identify and encourage players to attend the university. He set up a scholarship and financial aid program that was a combination of campus jobs and summer employment. And in 1937 Bible established an annual summer coaching school in cooperation with the Texas High School Football Coaches Association (THSFCA). He retired as the head coach at UT in 1946 after three SWC championships and then served as UT's athletic director for a decade, which allowed him time to write and publish his classic football book, *Championship Football: A Guide for Player, Coach and Fan* (1947).[6]

Stories are told that when D.X. was hired by Texas after leaving a championship Nebraska football program, more Texas Aggies than representatives from the Longhorns met him as he arrived at that train station in Austin. Bible's departure from A&M was seen as a great loss for the Aggies, and he was favorably remembered, except when he coached the Longhorns against the Aggies! The Texas A&M annual, titled *The Longhorn* until the cadets changed the name to *Aggieland* in 1949, remembered the man:

> D. X., as he is known to his men and friends, is a true gentleman of the old school. Quiet and unassuming, he has won the respect and admiration of those with whom he has come in contact. With his men, he is patient and friendly but is ever firm and always demands the higher type of sportsmanship, and it is through his leadership and example that Aggie teams have won such an enviable record for clean play and sportsmanship. He has won a place in the hearts of every Aggie and his name will live in the Hall of Fame of Aggieland.

Bible retired after thirty-four years coaching 297 collegiate games and winning 200 of them at five different universities; he won fourteen conference championships and his teams made three Cotton Bowl appearances.

Notwithstanding this tremendous career, when Coach Bible was asked to choose his greatest day in football, without hesitation he indicated the 1922 Dixie Classic victory: "We fought this game against terrific odds, and the achievement of winning is considered one of the greatest reversals of form in football history. Not our form, of course, for nobody except our own Aggie circle figured that anybody could dent the stonewall defenses and withstand the scoring onslaught of the little Kentucky college which had humbled great Harvard. This was not so much a game of thrills as of complete satisfaction to me, because I had full faith in the ability of the Aggies. They gave me my greatest day in football."[7]

In an interview by Tom Harrington in 1969, Coach Bible, reflecting on his years of coaching, concluded that in the Centre game, "our boys got ready" and it was "the finest victory I experienced during my career." Fifteen years after Bible zeroed in on the Dixie Classic as the most memorable moment in his coaching career, Kern Tips further confirmed the three major events of Bible's early career at Texas A&M: (1) the Aggie record of 1917–20; (2) the defeat of Centre College; and (3) the blazing aerial dogfight for the SWC championship between Joel Hunt of A&M and Gerald Mann of SMU.[8]

The numerous coaches and players who played with and for Bible and Moran would have an important impact on college athletics for decades, since many played and coached numerous sports, but they were particularly influential in football. The connections and relationships were remarkable. Former North Side High School and Centre College (1916–19) player Matty Bell departed TCU after being head coach for six seasons, from 1923–1928, finishing no higher than tied for third in the SWC, to become the coach at Texas A&M. After a very lackluster tenure of five years, he was relieved and considered retirement. But after a single year away from coaching he was hired by SMU, and during 1935, his first season, the Mustangs were SWC champions, going 12–0. In spite of a narrow loss to Stanford, 0–7, in the Rose Bowl, SMU was the first SWC team to play in Pasadena and was crowned the consensus national champion.[9]

Centre teammate Bo McMillin also headed into coaching. Within days of the Dixie Classic, Bo McMillin, after being courted to coach at numerous southern colleges as well as considering playing professional football, signed a three-year contract for $8,000 annually at tiny Centenary College, a liberal arts institution in Shreveport, Louisiana. In the 1920s coaching was becoming big business, and college stars such as McMillin, Matty Bell, and Knute Rockne were sought after by colleges who wanted winning programs. Furthermore, in the era of the organization of professional football and the nascent National Football League, there were no restrictions on coaching a college team on Saturday and playing in a professional game on Sunday. Bo routinely augmented his salary by pocketing between $500 to $2,000 per game playing occasionally for a number of pro teams. With the public's hunger for more football games, the rise of pro football was to have a major impact on college football and the rules determining amateur status.[10]

Centenary College had been crippled during World War I due to the loss of students and faculty. A group of Shreveport citizens agreed in 1921, with the backing of the college president, to subsidize Bo's salary. Bo, a master with the media and public relations, noted, "It is my ambition to have a winning football team at Centenary College, but it will be done in a clean, gentlemanly manner. We are going to live up to our name as 'Centenary Gentlemen' at all costs." In spite of having no coaching experience nor a college diploma, he was paid more than the college president and three times more than most of the faculty. The "star" quality of one of the leading players in the nation and a desire to field a winning team prevailed over all objections.

Although the college already had a young, capable coach named Homer H. Norton, the Centenary president wanted three things: instant gridiron success, increased enrollment, and expansion of the college's donor base. After only three seasons under Norton (1919–21), who had a 4–7 record, he was retained as an assistant coach and McMillin took over the football program in the summer of 1922.[11]

The Gents immediately went on to a series of victories, which preceded a gradual growth in the college's enrollment. McMillin would obtain a three-season record of 26–3, winning two Louisiana Intercollegiate Athletic championships. However, there was a growing concern that he did not adhere to the college's academic standards. As with his mentor Charlie Moran, McMillin's penchant for winning was questioned by detractors and opponents who complained about the coach's salary and lack of class attendance by his players. Once again, the Southern Association of Colleges weighed in, as it was considering accreditation for the college. This time the SAC stipulation was that the college would not be recognized unless McMillin was released. His contract was not renewed, and Centenary was granted membership. McMillin considered a return to Centre as head coach, but the college board could not agree on a salary increase after it was made clear by the Board of Trustees that "he would have to give up his professional Sabbath football."

When the NCAA failed to act on the conflict between amateur and professional football players (Red Grange bolted from Illinois University to sign a lucrative pro contract with the Chicago Bears), and following a number of fatal injuries and deaths (including the Waco Cotton Palace Riot of October 30, 1926, which resulted in the tragic killing of Texas Aggie cadet Charlie Sessums at halftime on Baylor's field), the American Association of University Professors (AAUP) weighed in. The academic organization delivered a scathing attack, reporting that football was creating a "hysteria" that was damaging to college education, further criticizing the vast sums of money being spent for coaches, players (in some cases), and new stadiums. But though the AAUP raised the level of concern, college football was solidly entrenched nationwide.

Before departing for Geneva College in Beaver Falls, Pennsylvania, Homer Norton was reinstated as the head coach at Centenary in 1926. Following a 27–5–1 record at Geneva, Bo coached at Kansas State and Indiana (1934–48), ending with an overall career record of 142–72–13. After his college coaching career he became the head coach of the NFL Detroit Lions from 1948 to 1950. He was inducted into the College Football Hall of Fame in 1951 and died in March 1952.[12]

Homer Norton inherited a great team from departing coach McMillin, and in his first two seasons back as head coach at Centenary, he won the league championship. After nine seasons at Centenary, compiling a record of 65–22–9, he was quietly approached about going to Texas A&M. Coming from a little college, he would be following three A&M coaching legends—Moran, Bible, and Matty Bell—but he was no stranger to playing the big colleges, having beaten Bible in 1928 and Matty Bell's Aggies in 1933 and 1934. Norton told his teams, "It's how you show up at the showdown that counts." Though he was very comfortable in Shreveport, in 1934 he nevertheless agreed to talk to Marion Church '08 and Joe Utay '08, who were representing the Texas A&M Athletic Council. They met at Utay's fishing cabin near Winona, Texas, and reached an agreement that was forwarded to the council and President T. O. Walton. Norton was hired at a salary of $8,000. He inherited an athletic program that was deeply in debt, a poor recruiting class, and no money to pay for assistant coaches, travel, or equipment. After three years of some creative financing to support the athletic department, rebuilding the team, and an aggressive recruiting program, Norton went after two dozen blue-chip high school players.

Colonel James Woodall '50, in his book *12 Texas Aggie War Heroes,* reviews Norton's plan to attract the top Texas players:

> Most were poor and could not go to A&M without a scholarship. The coach determined that he needed $25,000 to make his plan work. If he signed twenty-five players, he could provide scholarships that would cover each for four years. Norton contacted Bert Pfaff, a prominent former student who was a successful oilman and builder. Pfaff agreed to meet Norton and Lil Dimmitt, the Aggies' trainer and ace recruiter, at a Dallas bank. A bank officer thought Norton was there to make a payment on an outstanding loan and was surprised when the coach asked for a $25,000 loan. At first the banker refused, but when Pfaff threatened to close his account, the man relented and agreed to the loan.[13]

The first player signed was Marion "Dookie" Pugh, a quarterback from Fort Worth's North Side High School—the home of Centre College's legendary "Texas boys," led by Bo McMillin. The rest of the signees were a who's who of future college standouts, including Jim Thomason, Tommie Vaughn, Bill Miller, Chip Routt, John Kimbrough, and Marshall Robnett. This group would go on to a perfect undefeated and untied 11–0 season, beating Tulane, 14–13, in the 1939 Sugar Bowl to win Texas A&M's first national championship as ranked by the sportswriters of the Associated Press.[14]

With the win, the A&M Board of Directors approved a five-year contract extension and a pay raise for Coach Norton to $10,000. After two great seasons in 1940 (when the AP ranked A&M sixth) and 1941 (when the AP ranked them ninth), he remained at A&M through the 1947 season. The Aggies hosted both the 1941 and 1942 Cotton Bowls. However, after back-to-back losing seasons, the final two years of his contract were paid off, and he retired from coaching. Norton owned a popular restaurant on Texas Avenue, across from the main entrance to the campus. After Norton died in 1965 from a heart attack, D. X. Bible remembered him as a gentleman and competitor: "Texas is a better place because Homer Norton lived here."[15]

All-Southwest Conference halfback Sam Houston Sanders '22 also earned honors as captain on the Aggie track team, according to the 1922 *Longhorn,* with records in the 440 ("around 50 seconds flat") and high jump ("several inches higher than his head") as well as lettering in basketball. He was elected president of both his freshman and sophomore classes. After graduating in 1926 from the University of Tennessee Medical School in Memphis, he entered the practice of otolaryngology as an allergy specialist. He became a leading official in the old Southern Football Officials Association and organized the first program to recruit, train, and assign football officials for mid-South games. Dr. Sanders was the umpire in three Cotton Bowls, the 1941 Orange Bowl, and the 1942 Rose Bowl. Sanders was the major benefactor for the Sanders Corps of Cadets Center, museum, and conference center, built on the Texas A&M campus in 1992. He credited Coach Bible for giving him and many of his 1922 team members their career preparation, noting that Bible would tell them, "Give your all, and there shall be no regrets."[16]

Others who went on to coach include W. L. "Billy" Driver, a basketball coach and athletic director at Texas A&M with D. X. Bible, 1915–1920, and later the head coach at TCU. In his first season in 1920 with the Horned Frogs, his team went 9–0–1 and was named SWC champion. Local community excitement resulted in the first Southwest postseason bowl, the Fort Worth Classic. Moran, who returned home to Fort Worth with his Centre College team (starring six alumni of North Side High School), and Driver agreed that the game between TCU and Centre would be "no holds barred." The outcome was a lopsided Centre College win, 63–7.[17]

T. F. "Puny" Wilson '23, an end on the Aggie team in the Dixie Classic, earned four "T" letters and was All-Southwest Conference four successive years. He coached for thirty years, first briefly in professional football and then at Bryan (Texas) High School, at Allen Academy, and, beginning in 1938, at Sam Houston State Teachers' College in Huntsville. Famed as a punter from 1919 to 1922, Wilson punted twenty-three times in the 1922 Aggie-Longhorn game (which A&M won, 14–7), with an average punt of 55 yards. At Wilson's retirement at Sam Houston in 1952, Coach Bible said, "Puny Wilson was as great an end as I ever coached, a truly fine leader, and certainly was a contributor to what I call my greatest day in football, when the Aggies beat Centre. My, my, what a game Puny played that day." Puny also considered that day his greatest as a player.[18]

Warren "Rip" Collins '19 played professional baseball for eleven seasons, pitching for the New York Yankees, Detroit Tigers, Boston Red Sox, and St. Louis Browns, winning 108 games with a career ERA of 3.99. Rip's total professional salary from 1920 to 1931 was $58,900, with his highest take the $7,500 he earned pitching for the Tigers.

William C. "Heine" Weir '23 became dean and director of athletics at Schreiner Institute in Kerrville, Texas, and Asbury B. Morris '23 was a veteran of World War II and athletic director at Abilene Christian College.[19]

Bible's star running back from 1917 to 1919, Roswell G. "Little Hig" Higginbotham '19, returned to A&M to coach the freshman football team and serve as head coach of the baseball team, winning Texas A&M's first SWC baseball championship in 1931, followed by a second title in 1934. In 1936 he joined Matty Bell to coach at SMU. A World War I veteran, he returned to active duty in 1942 as a lieutenant (JG) in the US Navy; he died on active duty in 1943.

Little Hig's teammate Jack Mahan '21 was the first Aggie to compete in the Olympics, placing twelfth in the javelin throw at the 1920 Games at Antwerp, Belgium. W. G. "Bill" McMillan '22, who came off the bench to quarterback after A. B. Morris was injured in the Dixie Classic, returned to Lubbock after graduation to become a building contractor and owner of Westlake Golf Course. Bible noted, "Bill was a thoroughbred in every sense of the word, a leader, an imaginative quarterback, and my association with him as a player and since has been one of the fine experiences of coaching."[20]

JOE UTAY '08

Five decades after the Dixie Classic, I had a long talk with Joe Utay at his home in the Turtle Creek neighborhood in Dallas. He was modest about the role he played in organizing the first Dixie Classic, the forerunner of today's Cotton Bowl. He would have a profound impact on football in Texas for some six decades: he was one of the very few Texas athletes to not just play but also coach, officiate, and promote the game he loved. Sportswriter Kern Tips recalled, "By passion or design, Joe left A&M in 1908 deeply dedicated to football, not so much as a game but as an institution. With the instincts of an Indian scout and the determination of a trail boss, he assumed the responsibility of pulling and pushing football toward higher plateaus of recognition and accomplishment."

Joe, while a practicing attorney in Dallas, dedicated his activities to the promotion and expansion of college football. He officiated more than a hundred Southwest Conference games, including the last game Knute Rockne played for Notre Dame. In addition to being a founding member of the Texas A&M "T" Association, from 1915 to 1941 he was the southwest contributing editor for *Spalding Official Intercollegiate Foot Ball Guide.*

The 1922 Dixie Classic was considered a major success. Joe noted, "The net profit for the A&M–Centre College game was $1,000. We paid Centre $6,000." He never said what was paid to Texas A&M, but he reminded me with a smile that Georgia and Arkansas each received $750,000 for their participation in the 1976 Cotton Bowl game.[21]

The Dixie Classic (not to be confused with the Dixie Bowl, played in Birmingham, Alabama, in the 1940s) would be played two more times at Fair Park: in 1925 (West Virginia 9, SMU 7) and in 1934 (Arkansas 7, Centenary 7). As president of the Dixie Classic from 1929 to 1931, Joe Utay and the organizing committee altered the annual New Year's Day game format to an all-star game, pitting the Southwest Conference all-stars against the Big Ten all-stars, with the net receipts going to benefit the Texas Scottish Rite Hospital for Crippled Children. These games were the forerunner of the present-day Cotton Bowl, founded in 1937. An athletic committee with a representative from each member of the Southwest Conference (the first Texas A&M representative was E. J. Kyle) was established in 1936 to reorganize the Cotton Bowl with the SWC champion as the host team each year. Joe, author of the operational plans of the SWC–Cotton Bowl relationship going forward, was a member of the Cotton Bowl executive committee until 1974, at which time he was given a life membership. In 1941 the Southwest Conference Champions became the host team in the annual Cotton Bowl, with Texas A&M defeating Fordham University.[22]

But Joe Utay's attention was on more than football. In early May 1937, President Franklin D. Roosevelt, following a fishing trip in the Gulf of Mexico, boarded the presidential train in Galveston and, on his way back to Washington, stopped at the A&M College of Texas. A grand welcome was hosted at Kyle Field. All classes were canceled, and thousands from the surrounding communities flocked to the campus. One of FDR's primary reasons for stopping was to thank Texas A&M for the tremendous contributions by the college staff, students, and former students in World War I. During lunch in Sbisa Dining Hall, or perhaps on the reviewing stand prior to a review of the Corps, the president, following a comment that "it was a shame A&M did not have more dormitories," asked President Thomas O. Walton what could be done to assist A&M. Walton's answer: "More dorms." At this early date, FDR already was very aware of war clouds on the horizon, and an expansion of cadet officer production at A&M could be key to any future conflict. FDR's son Elliot, of Fort Worth, was a member of the A&M board of directors, along with Joe Utay and Robert W. "Bob" Briggs of Pharr.[23]

The prospect of assistance to finance the dorms was not forgotten, as Joe recalled: "FDR told Elliot to have a couple of board members come to Washington to get some money for dormitories. Elliot invited Bob and me to come to Washington that same week. When we got there, he told us the President and Mrs. R. had invited us to dinner Saturday, May 15, 1937." It took me a couple of years to locate the official White House purser's sign-in book from Hyde Park, New York, in FDR's presidential library. I also found records indicating that dinner was attended by A&M president Dr. T. O. Walton and Mr. and Mrs. James Roosevelt as well.[24]

Joe was very matter-of-fact about his visit to the White House. After dinner, Utay and Briggs met with Jesse Jones, famed Houston businessman and chairman of FDR's Reconstruction Finance Corporation (RFC), to arrange the procedure for a loan of $2 million to build twelve cadet dorms in the area to be known as the Quadrangle, or "Quad." Utay was designated to act as the attorney for the A&M Board and spent numerous days in Washington making the necessary arrangements to sort out the bureaucracy and expedite the construction loans. Dorm 12 in the Corps Quadrangle, built in 1940 (where I lived as a Squadron One "fish" in 1969–70), was named Joe Utay Hall in his honor.

One other very significant event that would have lasting impact on A&M was Joe's involvement in filling the vacant post of Commandant of Cadets at the college in 1937. While visiting Washington, the president referred him to the Chief of Staff of the Army in the War Department in order to find out what officers were available.

Joe recalls, "The Army Chief of Staff said he had a good man for the job, a young colonel named Moore. I asked the general, 'What is this colonel's first name?' The general answered, 'George.' 'George! He's my classmate, and we called him 'Maud!'"

This was indeed Col. George F. Moore '08, a guard and punter on the 1907 A&M team, whom they called Maud because he could kick a football like Maud the Mule, a well-known cartoon character of the era. Moore served as Commandant of Cadets from 1937 to 1940. He was a recognized builder of coastal fortifications and oversaw the building of the new A&M cadet dorms, the biggest construction project in the history of the college to that time. After completing two previous tours of duty in Manila improving

Newspaper cartoon noting Bible's 1922 victory over Centre College. (Source: Author's collections)

the fortifications there during the 1930s, he was recalled to regular active duty in 1941 as the commander and defender of Corregidor in the Philippines. At the height of the bombardment in mid-April 1942, General Moore ordered that a listing of all Texas Aggies on the Rock be compiled by his aide, Maj. Tom Dooley '35. The list and subsequent report would document the famous Texas Aggie Muster held on Corregidor in April 1942, just prior to the fall of the island.[25]

At the end of my interview with Joe, I asked his view on the Aggie spirit. Without hesitation he grinned and replied, "Once an Aggie, always an Aggie!"

The 1922 *Longhorn* was replete with references to the Dixie Classic and the impact of the victory on Texas Aggie football and the esprit de corps at the college. The victory was chronicled in a poem (see the appendix), and it was a clear editorial pleasure for the *Longhorn* staff to write about having their team beat Centre, billed as one of the two "Wonder Teams" of the early 1920s.

The Season's Latest Song Hit
"I Wonder! I Wonder!" sung by the University of Texas and Centre College. This song was sung at College Station Thanksgiving and at Dallas News Year's Day. Each time it was accompanied by a sixty-minute act by the Aggies entitled "Farmers Fight."

Farmers Fight
Farmers Fight, Farmers Fight!
Fight, Fight, Fight-Fight-Fight!
Tear 'um up! Smash 'em up!
Fight, Fight, Fight-Fight-Fight!
Farmers!
Farmers!
FIGHT!!![26]

As traditions are built over time, the legacy of the 12th Man has stood the test and is ingrained in the lore of Texas A&M. The event, innocuous at the time, of calling a student from the press box at a pivotal moment of the 1922 Dixie Classic would eventually make E. King Gill the image and icon of one of A&M's most enduring legacies. Indeed, to stand ready if called is at the heart of the spirit of the citizen-soldier and selfless service that has hallmarked generations of Aggie students and former students.

Joe Utay '08, captain of the 1907 A&M College team, was the founder of the January 1922 Dixie Classic in Dallas, the forerunner of the Cotton Bowl Classic. (Source: author's collection)

APPENDIX

The following poem was published in the 1922 Texas A&M yearbook, the *Longhorn,* celebrating the A&M victory over Centre College.

A Team There Was
A team there was and to Texas came,
Even as the Colonels did.
To play a game of national fame,
We called it a game, that would win us a name,
But the Colonels called it a practice game,
Even as Colonels can do.

Oh! The plays they knew and the things they'd do,
And the work of Bo and his dan,
"It's Gravy," said the Gink who slings pen and ink,
But not a single Gink would stop and think,
And of course, could not understand.

A team there was and their plays they tried,
Even as the Colonels did.
On passes and fakes and end runs they relied,
But most of them fell by the side,
And at the end of the game the score wasn't tied.
Even as the Colonels tried.

The Colonels were stripped of their world-wide fame,
Only as Colonels can be.
For they should have been when they entered that game,
That the "Texas Aggies," they could not tame,
But the Ginks said the Colonels were not to blame,
Even as Colonels can be.

Oh! There was no blame, and there was no shame,
To sting the Colonels like brands red hot,

For the Colonels knew full well,
That the Aggies gave them Hell,
And the Colonels were clearly outfought.

Coaches with Most Wins in College Football*

	Years	Wins	Losses	Ties	Percentage
Larry Kehres	27	322	24	3	92.9
John Gagliardi	61	489	138	11	77.3
Charles B. Moran**	18	122	3	12	76.6
Paul “Bear” Bryant**	37	323	85	17	76.0
Joe Paterno	45	409	135	3	74.4
Bobby Bowden	38	377	129	4	73.9
R. C. Slocum**	16	123	47	2	71.5
Glenn “Pop” Warner	35	318	106	32	69.7
Dana X. Bible**	34	190	71	22	67.7
Eddie Robinson	56	408	168	15	69.0
Amos Alonzo Stagg	56	329	190	35	59.3

*Includes all teams coached during career as head coach. No two reference lists of wins and losses are the same, and most individuals coached at multiple colleges. Disparities are the result of how number of games are counted and/or wins stripped from official records for NCAA violations and other matters outside the actual contests.

**Head coaches at Texas A&M; Bible’s winning record in 11 seasons at Texas A&M was 72–19–9, or 72 percent.

Notes

Introduction

1. On the 1920s as a golden age in college football, see, for example, Raymond Schmidt, *Shaping College Football: The Transformation of an American Sport, 1919–1930* (Syracuse: Syracuse University Press, 2007) and John M. Carroll, *Red Grange and the Rise of Modern Football* (Urbana: University of Illinois Press, 2004). For a contrary view, see William F. Freeman, "College Athletics in the Twenties: The Golden Age or Fool's Gold?," paper presented at the Symposium on the History of Sport and Physical Education, Seattle, WA, March 1977, available at https://files.eric.ed.gov/fulltext/ED175823.pdf.
2. "The A. and M. College," *Galveston Daily News,* February 27, 1893; "The A. & M. Nine Defeated by the Calvert Team," *Houston Post,* April 24, 1893; "Football," *Battalion,* October 15, 1893; November 1, 1893; December 1, 1893.
3. "Governor Aided A. and M. to Win," *Houston Post,* December 12, 1912.
4. For more on racially motivated violence in the Bryan, Texas, community generally, see Cynthia Nevels, *Lynching to Belong: Claiming Whiteness through Racial Violence* (College Station: Texas A&M University Press, 2007); for more on Klan activity in Texas during the period of this book, see Patricia Bernstein, *Ten Dollars to Hate: The Texas Man Who Fought the Klan* (College Station: Texas A&M University Press, 2017); for more on Klan activity and backgrounds generally, see Allen W. Trelease, *White Terror: The Ku Klux Klan Conspiracy and Southern Reconstruction* (Westport, CT: Praeger, 1979); and Bill Minutaglio, *A Single Star and Bloody Knuckles: A History of Politics and Race in Texas* (Austin: University of Texas Press, 2021), 110–11.

Chapter 1. Farmers Fight

1. "The State College," *Galveston Daily News,* June 25, 1878; "W. A. Trenckmann '78 [1878], Relates History of Early A. &. M. Days," *Texas Aggie,* December 15, 1926, 1; *The Olio,* 1895, 13–14, 23–33; *Longhorn,* 1907, 112–13; Walter Buenger and Walter Kamphoefner, eds., *Preserving German Texan Identity: Reminiscences of William A. Trenckmann, 1859–1935* (College Station: Texas A&M University Press, 2019), 10–11, 67–74, 198–204.
2. *Galveston Daily News,* June 27, 1878, and January 24, 1879. See also David Brooks Cofer, *First Five Administrations of Texas A. & M. College* (College Station: Association of Former Students, 1952).

3. John Adams, *We Are the Aggies* (College Station: Texas A&M University Press, 1979), 3–38.
4. *Galveston Daily News,* December 24, 1882, and July 19, 1883; "Sporting Topics," *Galveston Daily News,* November 6, 1894.
5. "Field Day Exercises," *Battalion,* 1893, 6.
6. "College String Band, "*College Journal,* January 1890, 16; Adams, *We Are the Aggies,* 15–22; John Adams, *Keepers of the Spirit: The Corps of Cadets at Texas A&M University* (College Station: Texas A&M University Press, 2001), 10–37.
7. "A. & M. College," *Galveston Daily News,* September 12, 1887, and June 9, 1889. See also Henry C. Dethloff, *The Centennial History of Texas A&M University 1876–1976* (College Station: Texas A&M University Press, 1975), 1:136–53.
8. "Called to a College," *Galveston Daily News,* July 6, 1890.
9. Dethloff, *Centennial History,* 1:154, 164–66; "A. & M. Graduates Greatly in Demand," n.d., Burgess Scrapbook, Cushing Library.
10. "The College Is Successful," *Galveston Daily News,* February 27, 1892; *A&M Annual Catalogue,* 1893, 56–57, and 1894, 67–68.
11. Edward Holick, "The Band: Texas A. and M. College," memo, May 7, 1954, and letter, John K. Woods to Tom, July 23, 1953, Texas Aggie Band File, Cushing Archives; "13 Members In First Band," *Battalion,* July 28, 1955.
12. "F. R. Ross President of Calliopean Society," *Battalion,* October 1, 1893; Adams, *Keepers of the Spirit,* 38–57. See also *The Olio,* 1895.
13. *Battalion,* October 1, 1893, May 1894, and December 1894.
14. "Intercollegiate Football," *New York Times,* October 28, 1887.
15. "'Bob' Littlejohn First A. & M. Coach," *Fort Worth Star-Telegram,* November 17, 1909; *A&M Catalogue,* 1892, 17. See also Wilbur Evans and H. B. McElroy, *The Twelfth Man: A Story of Texas A&M Football* (Huntsville, AL: Strode, 1974), 23–29; Kern Tips, *Football—Texas Style* (New York: Doubleday, 1964), 1–5.
16. *Battalion,* November 1, 1893, and December 1893; "The A. and M. College," *Galveston Daily News,* February 27, 1893. Football uniforms were ordered, but there is no detail of their description.
17. "A. and M. College," *Battalion,* January 29, 1894; "Gone Football Mad," *Galveston Daily News,* October 28, 1894, and February 19, 1894.
18. *Galveston Daily News,* October 21, 1894, and November 3, 1894; *Fort Worth Daily Gazette,* October 21, 1894.
19. "Was Football Day: The Ball High School Boys Defeated by the A. & M. College Eleven," *Galveston Daily News,* November 30, 1894; "A. and M. College," *Galveston Daily News,* November 6, 1893; "As to Football," *Galveston Daily News,* December 4, 1894. The average weight of a Ball High player was 145 pounds; the average weight of an A&M player was 152 pounds.

20. "A. and M. College," *Galveston Daily News,* October 19, 1896; "A Word as to Football," *Galveston Daily News,* October 26, 1897; *Longhorn,* 1911, 191: "Athletic Sports," *A&M Annual Catalogue,* 1902–3, 70.
21. Minutes of the Texas A&M board of directors, December 10, 1901; Minutes of the Association of Former Students, June 9, 1902, I:24, Cushing Archives.
22. Minutes of the Association of Former Students, June 8, 1903, I:26; *Galveston Daily News,* November 28, 29, 1902; *Dallas News,* December 29, 1902; *Longhorn,* 1903, 45; Arthur P. Watts, "The Romantic Days of the Flying Wedge," *Dallas Morning News,* November 17, 1929; Adams, *We Are the Aggies,* 53.
23. *The Contribution of Edwin J. Kyle to the Development of the Athletic Program of the Agricultural and Mechanical College of Texas* (Houston: Adco Press, 1952), 1–21; David Chapman, "The Kyle Field Chronicle," in four parts, *Texas Aggie,* April, June, August, and October 1996. In March 1909, the grandstand from the Bryan Fair Association was purchased and moved to Kyle Field.
24. *Longhorn,* 1909, 138; "A History of A. and M. College," *Houston Daily Post,* June 6, 1909. Charter members of the SIAA were Texas A&M, Baylor, Southwestern, Texas, Trinity, and Austin College. Fort Worth University, Oklahoma, Washington University, and Missouri School of Mines joined later.

Chapter 2. Moran and Bible

1. Caesar Hohn, *Dutchman on the Brazos: Reminiscences of Caesar "Dutch" Hohn* (Austin: University of Texas Press, 1963), 69.
2. Glenn S. Warner, *Football for Coaches and Players* (1927; reprint, Carlisle, PA: Tuxedo Press, 2007).
3. Hohn, *Dutchman on the Brazos,* 57. Dutch Hohn was the captain for the 1911 football team.
4. Hohn, *Dutchman on the Brazos,* 60, 80; Barbara Donaldson, *Kyle Tough* (Bryan: The Oaks Press, 2003), 85, 92–93; Wilbur Evans and H. B. McElroy, *The Twelfth Man: A Story of Texas A&M Football* (Huntsville, AL: Strode, 1974), 58–62; "A. & M. Football Outlook," *Dallas Morning News,* September 12, 1909; "A. & M Won Brilliant Victory over Varsity on Muddy Field," *Houston Chronicle,* November 8, 1909 ("Charlie" is spelled three different ways, including "Charley" and "Charly").
5. "A. & M. 5—Varsity 0," *Bryan Eagle,* December 2, 1909. A letter from Sam A. McMillan to David Cofer captures the emerging traditions and "college spirit" under Moran: "Old traditions were fading away and new ones were taking form. We saw that sacred cow 'college spirit' grow from a wobbly calf to a creature larger and wilder than Paul Bunyan's Blue Ox. The green turf from Charlie Moran's 'win at any cost' football games had a growth stimulus, for it compared with that to which an elephant's milk was like branch water.

Why football hysteria should so suddenly dominate the enduring and worthwhile features of A. and M. activities puzzles everyone who takes the trouble to think about it." David B. Cofer, *Fragments of Early History of the Texas A. and M. College* (College Station: Association of Former Students, 1953), 88.

6. "With the Athletics at A. and M. College," *Galveston Daily News,* April 10, 1911; Cofer, *Fragments of Early History,* 31; "Latest Sporting News," *Fort Worth Star-Telegram,* October 17, 1911; Hohn, *Dutchman on the Brazos,* 59; Donalson, *Kyle Tough,* 86; interview with Bill Page '76, October 2, 2019. See also John Adams, *Keepers of the Spirit.*
7. Hohn, *Dutchman on the Brazos,* 74–77; John J. Miller, *The Big Scrum: How Teddy Roosevelt Saved Football* (New York: Harper, 2011), 174–210.
8. Hohn, *Dutchman on the Brazos,* 61.
9. "Charley Moran Named as Next Year's A. & M. Coach," *Fort Worth Star-Telegram,* May 18, 1914; John S. Watterson, *College Football* (Baltimore: John Hopkins University Press, 2000), 67.
10. "Yale Man Helps Moran with Aggies, Andrews Has Been Signed as Assistant Coach—Training Camp on Gulf Coast," *Fort Worth Star-Telegram,* August 8, 1910; "Training Will Begin Monday," *San Antonio Daily Express,* September 11, 1910. Bill Page '76 has compiled an extensive record of the Aggie preseason camps; see "Football Training Camps, 1910–1914," Cushing Archives. See also Jim Dent, *The Junction Boys* (New York: St. Martin's Press, 1999).
11. "Texas A. & M. Has Good Eleven," *El Paso Herald,* September 15, 1910; "Seabrook Training Camp," *Dallas Morning News,* September 16, 1910; Hohn, *Dutchman on the Brazos,* 72–74.
12. "Seabrook Training: 'Pull Yourselves In, Boys,'" *Houston Daily Post,* September 18, 1910; *Longhorn,* 1911, 199–201. Dana Bible recalled, "You played with the shape of the football that best suited the fancy of the home team—at one place the ball might be slim and light, the next place more spherical, discouraging forward passes." Quoted in Ty Cashion, *Pigskin Pulpit: A Social History of Texas High School Football Coaches* (Austin: TSHA, 1998), 52.
13. "Seabrook, Texas," *Houston Daily Post,* September 19 and 21, 1910; "A. & M. Football Squad Boasts of Many Stars," *Fort Worth Star-Telegram,* September 20, 1910; *Longhorn,* 1912, 259–60.
14. Contract, Texas A&M Athletic Association with Joe Utay, College Station, July 29, 1912, Utay Papers, Cushing Archives.
15. "Open Sylvan Beach Camp," *Houston Daily Post,* September 10, 1911; "A. and M. Squad at La Porte," *Austin Statesman,* September 17, 1911; "A. &. M. Expects Moran to Arrive Today," *Houston Post,* September 12, 1912; "Farm-

ers Report Soon," *Bryan Daily Eagle and Pilot,* September 1, 1913; "Aggie Will Train at Ott Sen's Farm," *Dallas Morning News,* August 24, 1914; "Recent Scenes at Aggies Camp at Stang," *Dallas Morning News,* September 27, 1914; *A&M Catalogue,* 1910, 2; *A&M Catalogue,* 1911, 4. A&M classes began on Tuesday, September 27 in 1910, and on Tuesday, September 26 in 1911.

16. "Farmers Won on Slushy Field," *Bryan Eagle,* December 3, 1914; "Coach C. B. Moran Resigns at A. M." *Bryan Eagle,* December 17, 1914; *Waco Daily Times Herald,* November 10, 1908; "Dress Parade and Many Marks of Respect Shown for Retiring Athletic Director," *Houston Post,* December 18, 1914; John D. Forsyth, *The Aggies and the Horns* (Austin: Texas Monthly Press, 1981), 30. See also *Longhorn,* 1910, 184–86.
17. *Shrapnel,* January 1915, 1–23; "Moran Given Sendoff at Texas A. & M.," *Fort Worth Star-Telegram,* December 19, 1914; Hohn, *Dutchman on the Brazos,* 68–69; Donalson, *Kyle Tough,* 88, 109 ; Evans and McElroy, *Twelfth Man,* 58–62. The new SWC was composed of Texas A&M, Arkansas, Baylor, Oklahoma A&M, Texas, University of Oklahoma, Rice, and Southwestern University.
18. Evans and McElroy, *Twelfth Man,* 58–62. Note: The new SWC was composed of Texas A&M, Arkansas, Baylor, Oklahoma A&M, Texas, University of Oklahoma, Rice, and Southwestern University.
19. Interview with Joe Utay '08, May 21, 1976; "A Texas–A. &. M. Games," *Austin Statesman,* February 28, 1914; "A&M–TU Rivalry Broke Up for Four Years after 1911 Tussle," *Bryan Eagle,* October 3, 1950. See also "Charley Moran Named as Next Year's A. & M. Coach," *Fort Worth Star-Telegram,* May 18, 1914; Warfield, *Aggies: A Century of Football Tradition,* 22–23, 26–27, 30–31.
20. Dethloff, *Centennial History,* 1:258–59. See also "Early Steer–Aggie Tilts Recalled by Moran's Death," *San Antonio Express News,* June 16, 1949.
21. Ike Ashburn, "D. X. Bible: The Man Who Kept His Feet on the Ground," *Parade Magazine,* January 1955, 8, 18; Cohane, *Great College Football Coaches of the Twenties and Thirties* (New Rochelle: Arlington House, 1973), 28–29.
22. Cashion, *Pigskin Pulpit,* 49–56; Pamela W. Johnson, *The Corps: The CORE of A&M* (College Station: Privately published, 2017), 19–23.
23. Johnson, *Corps,* 29; *Longhorn,* 1917, n.p.
24. "A. & M. Gets Ready for Huge Crowd," *Fort Worth Star-Telegram,* October 10, 1915; "Longhorns Beaten by Texas Farmers," *Dallas Morning News,* November 20, 1915; Evans and McElroy, *Twelfth Man,* 71; "The Freshman Squad," *Longhorn,* 1916, 243, 258–61; "Bible Replaces Eddie Harlan," *Houston Post,* December 24, 1916. The exact reason for Harlan's departure is unclear. At

Princeton he had been team captain and quarterback and twice selected as an All-American; after graduation he coached for a time at Pittsburgh before coming to Texas A&M.

25. "Texas 'Aggies' 1917 Southwest Champions," *Alumni Quarterly,* February 1918, 3–4, 24; *Longhorn,* 1918, 338–350; Publicity Department, "Fifty Facts about the Agricultural & Mechanical College of Texas," College Station, October 11, 1915, Cushing Archives.
26. Charles Puryear, "The War and the College," *Alumni Quarterly,* November 1918, 3–4; John A. Adams Jr., *Over There in the Air: The Fightin' Texas Aggies in World War I, 1917-1918* (College Station: Texas A&M University Press, 2019), 18–22.
27. "Coach Bible Has Become an Aviator," *Houston Post,* January 6, 1918; "Champions of the Southwest," *Longhorn,* 1918, 340; Cohane, *Great College Football Coaches,* 25; Bible Draft Registration Card, Brazos County Records; Henry C. Dethloff, *Texas Aggies Go to War* (College Station: Texas A&M University Press, 2006), 37–62.
28. "Coach D. V. Graves," *Longhorn,* 1919, 147, 152; "The Captains of the Four Major Sports for 1918–1919 Session Are in the Service," *Alumni Quarterly,* November 1918, 19; *Longhorn,* 1919, 147; Athletic Report, *21st Biennial Report of A. and M. College of Texas,* College Station, period ending August 1918, 110–11.
29. "D. X. Bible: A 10-Year Man at A&M," *Austin Statesman,* November 29, 1928; Ike Ashburn, "D. X. Bible," *Texas Parade,* January 1955, 8; Dana X. Bible US Army discharge papers, Cushing Archives, Form No. 724-2 A.G.O., honorable discharge, July 8, 1918; David M. Nelson, *The Anatomy of a Game: Football, the Rules, and Men Who Made the Game* (Newark: University of Delaware Press, 2021), 169–71. The official discharge listed as his residence "Athletic Dept—College Station," and incorrectly stated his birthplace was Jefferson City, Texas, where in fact it should have stated Tennessee.
30. Anonymous verse seen in Nelson, *Anatomy of a Game,* 171.
31. Clarence G. Barth, *History of the Twentieth Aero Squadron* (reprint; Nashville: Battery Press, 1990), 50–51; "D. X. Bible Will Soon Be Back at College," *The Reveille,* March 30, 1919, 1; "Coach Bible Back," *Alumni Quarterly,* May 1919, 14; "D. X. Bible," *Alumni Quarterly,* August 1918, 26; "D. X. Bible," *Longhorn,* 1920, 359, 384. See also Bill Page '76, ed., "When Aggieland Turned Khaki: World War I at Texas A&M," College Station, July 16, 2016, unpublished manuscript, Cushing Archives. D. V. Graves remained as an assistant football coach and was joined by former Alabama head coach W. L. Driver.
32. "Texas A&M Celebrates Black History and Achievement," *Texas A&M Today,* January 31, 2020, available at https://today.tamu.edu/2013/08/27/texas-am

-to-commemorate-50th-anniversary-of-admission-of-women-minority-inclusiveness/; "Texas A&M to Commemorate 50th Anniversary of Admission of Woman, Minority Inclusiveness," *Texas A&M Today,* August 27, 2013, available at https://today.tamu.edu/2013/08/27/texas-am-to-commemorate-50th-anniversary-of-admission-of-women-minority-inclusiveness/.

33. Jordan Burnham, "Facing A&M's Past," *Battalion,* February 28, 2019, available at http://www.thebatt.com/news/facing-a-m-s-past/article_b95f6fb2-3b2b-11e9-ba89-0b1d134044d0.html.
34. D. X. Bible to H. C. Dillingham, August 19, 1921, Bible Papers, Cushing Archives. The motto "They shall not pass" was a World War I slogan used to express determination to defend a position against an enemy—most famously used during the Battle of Verdun, "Ils ne passeront pas!" Also worth mentioning is that recruiting letters of this era were often very interesting, in an effort to attract the attention of prospective players. Coach Robert Myers, at Centre, sent the following, in part: "Wouldn't you like to be prancing around in our big new stadium right now. We have a houseful of good football equipment and plenty of new stuff coming in. Big boy, our freshman are game enough to climb naked up a honey-locust tree with a wildcat under each arm; they'd fight a shark on the bottom of the ocean with an anvil in each hand, or get hair-singe under a gasoline shower. I guarantee you'll have the time of your young life on Centre's yearling football team. Meanwhile get set to be with us for there are wonderful things ahead for you."
35. *Longhorn,* 1920, 359, 371, 382–84; "Football Prospects," *Bryan Daily Eagle,* August 19, 1919; "Success of Athletics," *Bryan Daily Eagle,* June 20, 1921; *Longhorn,* 1921, 357, 363.
36. Official program, Harvard vs. Centre, Soldiers Field, October 29, 1921, Centre College Archives. See also Watterson, *College Football,* 137–47.
37. For the historical evolution of college football rules, see Nelson, *Anatomy of a Game,* 433–532.
38. *Longhorn,* 1916, 259; *Longhorn,* 1921, 357, 366.
39. "Improvements in Aggie Athletics," *Dallas Morning News,* August 23, 1922; Watterson, *College Football,* 135–47; Dave Revsine, *The Opening Kickoff* (Guilford: Lyons Press, 2014), 196–99.
40. Dana X. Bible, *Championship Football: A Guide for Player, Coach and Fan* (New York: Prentice Hall, 1947), 130.
41. Interview with Joe Utay '08, May 21, 1976.

Chapter 3. The Classic Game

1. Interview with Joe Utay '08 at Turtle Creek, Dallas, May 21, 1976, and letter from Utay, June 14, 1976; *Longhorn,* 1908, 161–62; "A. and M. Men Organize Cavalry Regiment," *Alumni Quarterly,* February 1918, 12, and May 1918, 15; "A. and M. Regiment Is Ready for Federalization," *Alumni Quarterly,*

November 1918, 10. Utay's 1909 Holy Trinity team won the championship of the North Texas Interscholastic Association, and his overall record was 15–7–1. Also, Utay was the referee in the last game Knute Rockne played at Notre Dame.

2. Robert W. Robertson, *The Wonder Team: The Story of the Centre College Praying Colonels* (Louisville: Butler Books, 2008), 172–78, 376–78.
3. Robertson, *Wonder Team,* 172–73, 372–79. During the 1919 season, TCU had only one win and scored only 20 points (three touchdowns) during their eight-game campaign under first-year head coach Ted Hackney.
4. Dana Bible, "Dixie Classic," in Murray Goodman and Leonard Lewin, *My Greatest Day in Football* (New York: A. S. Barnes, 1948), 31–35; Robertson, *Wonder Team,* 336–38.
5. "Bo and Mates," seen in Robertson, *Wonder Team,* 363–64.
6. Robertson, *Wonder Team,* 11–12.
7. Charles W. Akers and John W. Carter, *Bo McMillin: Man and Legend* (Louisville: Sulgrave Press, 1989), 2–10; Harold Ratliff, *Autumn's Mightiest Legions: History of Texas Schoolboy Football* (Waco: Texian Press, 1963), 10; Cashion, *Pigskin Pulpit,* 54–55.
8. Earl Ruby, "Ruby's Report: Bo McMillin Went to Centre Via Somerset," *Courier-Journal,* 1952, Moran Clippings File, Centre College Archives.
9. Robertson, *Wonder Team,* 19. See also Akers and Carter, *Bo McMillin,* 24–26.
10. Akers and Carter, *Bo McMillin,* 64.
11. Robertson, *Wonder Team,* 23–28.
12. "The Praying Football Team," *Literary Digest,* December 11, 1920, 39; Allison Danzig, *The History of American Football: Its Great Teams, Players, and Coaches* (Englewood Cliffs: Prentice-Hall, 1956), 235–36.
13. Robertson, *Wonder Team,* 68–70; Akers and Carter, *Bo McMillin,* 36–37.
14. Texas A&M would not have its first All-American in football until 1937, when Joe Routt was selected; he repeated the honor in 1938. As a captain in the US Army, he was killed in action at the Battle of the Bulge in late 1944.
15. "Old Centre Wins!," *Lexington Daily Leader,* October 30, 1921; Robertson, *Wonder Team,* 250–74; "Former Aggie Coach Now with Center [*sic*] College Kentucky," *Alumni Quarterly,* February 1920, 15; "Charlie Moran" and "A. and M. Roots as Charles Licks Them," *Texas Aggies,* November 1, 1921, 1; Akers and Carter, *Bo McMillin,* 57–65.
16. Wilbur Evans and H. B. McElroy, *The Twelfth Man: A Story of Texas A&M Football* (Huntsville, AL: Strode, 1974), 84.
17. "Aggies Are Given Appropriate Song," *Daily Bulletin,* October 1, 1925, refers to the introduction of the song "Spirit of Aggieland," yet clearly states that the fight song to date was titled "Goodbye to Texas University." Second verse, written by Pinky Wilson, was introduced in 1938; "War Hymn," *Battalion,* December 9, 1938.

18. Interview with James Vernon "Pinky" Wilson '20, Burnet, Texas, March 19, 1975; Jeff Dunn '76, "A History of the Texas A&M Football Fight Songs: 1902–1950," presentation, College Station, October 21, 2016; Adams, *We Are the Aggies,* 118–20.
19. "Southwest Champions Bring Wonder Team Here to Battle Vandy Eleven," *Dallas Morning News,* October 16, 1921.
20. "The Wonder Team Wonders How It Happened," *Longhorn,* 1922, 367–68. The term "wonder" must have been a much-used accolade, as the Texas team and Centre received equal billing during the 1921 football season.
21. Evans and McElroy, *Twelfth Man,* 12–14.
22. "California Ready for W. and J. Game," *Dallas Morning News,* January 1, 1922; "East-West Battle Ends in 0–0 Score," *New York Times,* January 2, 1922; Kern Tips, *Football—Texas Style* (New York: Doubleday, 1964), 211.
23. Douglas MacArthur to Joseph Utay, December 9, 1921, Utay Papers, Cushing Archives. See also "D. X. Bible Returns Home from France," *Battalion,* April 2, 1919.
24. Interview with Joe Utay '08, May 21, 1976; "Centre," *New York Times,* November 21, 1921; Robertson, *Wonder Team,* 351–79; John S. Watterson, *College Football* (Baltimore: John Hopkins University Press, 2000), 143–44; John Adams, *Keepers of the Spirit,* 126. In early December 1921, before they knew Utay had signed Centre to come to Dallas, Houston sports promoters and "enthusiasts" attempted to arrange a postseason game between Baylor and Centre in Houston for January 2. Baylor declined because they said they had to prepare for basketball season. See "Baylor Declines Game with Centre College at Houston Jan. 2," *Austin Statesman,* December 2, 1921.
25. Watterson, *College Football,* 371–73.
26. "Floyd Buckner Returns to College," *Weatherford Daily Herald,* January 9, 1922.
27. Dana X. Bible, *Championship Football: A Guide for Player, Coach and Fan* (New York: Prentice Hall, 1947), 3–5.
28. "Aggie Defense on Trial Today," *San Antonio Express News,* January 2, 1922; "Centre Is Favorite to Win Battle" and "Get Together Is Banquet Spirit," *Dallas Morning News,* January 2, 1922; "Centre- A. & M. Game Draws 12,000 Advance," *Austin Statesman,* January 2, 1922; Goodman and Lewin, *My Greatest Day in Football,* 33; "Moran's Men Reveled While Aggies Slept," *San Antonio Express,* January 3, 1922.
29. Cohane, *Great College Football Coaches,* 26–29; Nelson, *The Anatomy of a Game,* 172; Richard White, *The Republic for Which It Stands* (New York: Oxford University Press, 2017), 726.
30. "Bo McMillin Married," *New York Times,* January 3, 1922; Robertson, *Wonder Team,* 375–77; "Miss Marie Miers," *Washington Post,* January 3, 1922.
31. Robertson, *Wonder Team,* 378.

32. Evans and McElroy, *Twelfth Man*, 86–88.
33. "Dallas Contribution to Aggies' First String Line-up," *Dallas Morning News*, January 1, 1922.
34. "Game to Be Reported at Pavilion" and "Football Reports Will Be Received Here by Wireless," *Daily Bulletin*, October 8, 1920; "Farmers Defeat the Oklahomans 35 to 0," *Daily Bulletin*, November 1, 1920; letter, W. B. Bizzell to D. J. Finn, October 13, 1920, D. J. Finn and City National Bank check number 19, Finn to Bryan Telephone Co., October 30, 1920, Scrapbook, Cushing Archives; "Prof Remembers First Grid Broadcast," *Battalion*, November 16, 1962.
35. "Sidelights on A&M. Game," *Austin Statesman*, November 25, 1921; James O. Smith, *Modern Radio Operations* (New York: Wireless Press, 1922), 89; Charles R. Schultz, "First Aggie Football Broadcast," *Texas Aggie*, November 1993, 37; Evans and McElroy, *Twelfth Man*, 91. Prior to the Dallas game, the promoters in the Wallace Building had set up some six hundred seats prior to the December 17, 1921 state high school championship in Austin between Bryan High and Oak Cliff High of Dallas, a dry run of their system prior to the Dixie Classic; see "See the Bryan-Oak Cliff Football Game," *Bryan Eagle*, December 16, 1921.
36. *Longhorn*, 1922, 367; "Centre's Wonder Team Falls," *San Antonio Express*, January 3, 1922; "Aggie Triumphs," *Houston Post*, January 3, 1922.
37. "Bible on Nat'l Rules Committee," *Texas Aggie*, January 15, 1922; Nelson, *Anatomy of a Game*, 192, 533.
38. Tips, *Football—Texas Style*, 213. Immediately after the win over Centre, Bible wired his dad, Squire Bible, "Papa, my A&M team whipped the praying colonels insuring us the rating of the national football champions and I learned today of my appointment on the National Football Rules Committee." Squire, a professor of philosophy, wired back simply: "Son keep your feet on the ground." See Ashburn, "D. X. Bible," *Parade*, January 1955, 8.
39. William B. Ruggles, "Texas Aggies Defeat Victorious Colonels," *Bryan Eagle*, January 3, 1922; *Longhorn*, 1922, 369–70.
40. Nelson, *Anatomy of a Game*, 473.
41. William B. Ruggles, "Roberts Fails to Play Stellar Role," *Dallas Morning News*, January 3, 1922; "Play by Play," *Houston Post*, January 3, 1922.
42. Robertson, *Wonder Team*, 378–79.
43. Associated Press, "Play by Play," *Houston Post*, January 3, 1922; AP, "Centre's Wonder Team Falls Before Attack of Texas A&M," *San Antonio Express*, January 3, 1922.
44. Smylie, "A&M's First 'Twelfth Man,'" *Houston Press*, January 19, 1956.
45. Goodman and Lewin, *My Greatest Day in Football*, 34–35; "A&M Defeats Centre with 22–14 Score," *Austin American Statesman*, January 3, 1922; *Longhorn*, 1922, 269–70.

46. "Texas Defeat Is Lesson to Centre," n.d., Moran Clippings File, Centre College Archives; Robertson, *Wonder Team,* 381; Robert W. Maxwell, "Better Eleven Wins When Texans Spring Surprise on Centre," *Texas Aggie,* January 15, 1922.
47. "Coach Bible Pays Tribute to Aggies," *Bryan Eagle,* January 3, 1922; Horace S. McCoy, "Play by Play Story of Game Pays Great Tribute to Aggie Team," *Texas Aggie,* January 15, 1922.
48. *Longhorn,* 1922, 3–4 ("Dedication to Dana X. Bible—Source of Aggie faith—One of the greatest football coaches of his day, whose clean spirit of fight has won him a great name in America and a greater place in the hearts of all men of A. & M., this volume of the Longhorn is Dedicated"), 370; "Praying Colonels Downed by Texans," *New York Times,* January 3, 1922; "Taps!," *Boston Post,* January 3, 1922, reprinted in the *Texas Aggie,* January 15, 1922.
49. *Texas Aggie,* January 15, 1922; "A. & M. Defeats Centre: Texans Outplay Praying Colonels," *Austin American Statesman,* January 3, 1922; "'Praying Colonels' Very Meek," *Los Angeles Times,* January 4, 1922.
50. Program, Football Texas A. & M. College versus Centre College, January 2, 1922, 3: "Texas Aggies Smear Centre Eleven, 22–14," *Chicago Tribune,* January 3, 1922; "Praying Colonels Downed by Texans," *New York Times,* January 3, 1922.
51. Quote in Evans and McElroy, *Twelfth Man,* 85; "Aggie Victory Live Topic in Sports World," *Battalion,* January 13, 1922; Harold Ratliff, *"I Shook the Hand . . ."* (San Antonio: Naylor, 1948), 34.
52. Evans and McElroy, *Twelfth Man,* 86–87; Ross Tenney, "Much Dissatisfaction over Walter Camp's All-American Team: Football Dean Is Accused of Favoring East," *Des Moines Capital,* December 31, 1922; *Longhorn,* 1922, 370. The Maxwell Trophy is presented annually to the best all-around player, selected by sportswriters, sports broadcasters, and NCAA head coaches.
53. Joe Utay, "Southwestern Conference Foot Ball," in *Spalding's Intercollegiate Foot Ball Guide,* ed. Walter Camp (New York: American Sports Publishing, 1922), 75, 77; "Tributes from Bible and Quigley," *Houston Post,* January 20, 1952; "Jinx Tucker's Hot Shots on the Texas Aggie–Centre Game," reprinted from the *Waco News-Tribune* in the *Texas Aggie,* January 15, 1922.
54. Danzig, *The History of American Football,* 45–46; Tips, *Football—Texas Style,* 21.
55. "No All-Americans for 1922," *Battalion,* February 10, 1922; "All-American Teams of East Are Jokes: Critics Who Never Saw a Western Team Play to Name Best in Country," *Mansfield News,* December 8, 1910. SMU played in their first bowl game in the 1924 Dixie Classic, losing to West Virginia, 7–9.

Chapter 4. The 12th Man

1. https://soundcloud.com/user-607700520/the-story-of-the-12th-man; E. King Gill Papers, Cushing Archives; Dana X. Bible, audio file, 060980, Cushing Archives. See also David Chapman, "Dr. E. King Gill '24: Original 12th Man," *Texas Aggie,* January 1995, 15, and John Adams, "A&M Traditions Often Comical, Always Unique," *Battalion,* August 25, 1976.
2. Vernon Smylie, "A&M's First 'Twelfth Man,'" *Houston Press,* January 19, 1956.
3. *Longhorn,* 1922, 360; game-day program, "Football Texas A & M. College versus Centre College," January 2, 1922, Dallas, 5–7.
4. Smylie, "A&M's First 'Twelfth Man.'"
5. Kern Tips, *Football—Texas Style* (New York: Doubleday, 1964), 213. See also R. E. "Peppy" Blount, *Mamas, Don't Let Your Babies Grow Up to Play Football* (Austin: Eakin Press, 1985), 39.
6. Jerry C. Cooper, *Here: The Muster Speeches at Texas A&M University* (College Station: Texas A&M University Press, 2013), 246; Robertson, *Wonder Team,* 384–85; Wilbur Evans and H. B. McElroy, *The Twelfth Man: A Story of Texas A&M Football* (Huntsville, AL: Strode, 1974), 17–18; "Mac's Facts: M. G. McMillan," *Lubbock Morning Avalanche,* April 30, 1958.
7. Editorial, *Battalion,* October 24, 1923, and October 24, 1924. See also T. G. Webb, *Battle of the Brazos* (College Station: Texas A&M University Press, 2018).
8. "To the Corps," *Battalion,* November 26, 1924.
9. Mervin Stephens, "Aggies Show Proper Fighting Spirit in Practice for Game with Sewanee at Dallas Fair," *Bryan Eagle,* October 7, 1925; "Sewanee Fails Fourth Time to Best Farmers," *Battalion,* October 13, 1926.
10. "Aggies, Denied Victory over TCU Since '24," *Galveston Daily News,* October 15, 1933; "Campus Combings," *Galveston Daily News,* December 3, 1933.
11. Interview with E. E. McQuillen '20, June 2, 1975; "NBC Will Feature Sugar Bowl," *Battalion,* December 14, 1939; "'Aggie War Hymn' to be Broadcast of Kraft," *Battalion,* November 2, 1939; Barbara Donaldson, *Kyle Tough: The Saga of Texas A&M's Rise to Power in Athletics and Agriculture* (Bryan: Oak Press, 2003), 231–35; Joseph G. Rollins, *"Aggies Y'all Caught That Dam' Ol' Rat Yet?"* (San Antonio: Naylor, 1970), 49–51; Mickey Herskowitz, "Glory Aggies of 1920 Looking to Tuesday," *Houston Post,* January 17, 1960.
12. Voice recording of E. King Gill, www.aggienetwork.com/news/152458/12th-man-story, April 21, 1964; interview with Robert A. Epstein '44, February 10, 2020; *Longhorn,* 1922, 358, 380, 384; John A. Adams, *Softly Call the Muster: The Evolution of a Texas Aggie Tradition* (College Station: Texas A&M University Press, 1979), xxi, 25–51; Robert Epstein '44, "Reflections on the 1946 Corregidor Muster," remarks at the dedication of the Texas Aggie Memorial on the main drill field "Top-side on the Rock" at Corregidor,

Manila Bay, April 21, 2015, transcribed by John Adams '73. See also Adams, *The Fightin' Texas Aggie Defenders of Bataan and Corregidor* (College Station: Texas A&M University Press, 2016).

13. "'The Twelfth Man' New Song of Corps Presented Tuesday," *Battalion,* September 18, 21, 1941; "Aggies Look to Twelfth Man," *Amarillo Daily News,* September 30, 1941; "Like One Student All Aggies Call Themselves the 12th Man," *Houston Post,* November 11, 1942.
14. Lloyd Gregory, "When Texas Aggies Defeated Centre in the Forerunner to Cotton Bowl," *Houston Post,* January 3, 1943; Mickey Herskowitz, *The 1939 Texas Aggies: The Greatest Generation's Greatest Team* (Houston: Halcyon Press, 2006), 221–22; Henry C. Dethloff, *The Centennial History of Texas A&M University 1876–1976* (College Station: Texas A&M University Press, 1975), 2:476–79; Donaldson, *Kyle Tough,* 271–73; "Gill Put Aggies on Their Feet," *Austin Statesman,* April 1, 1944; "The Origin of Aggie 'Twelfth Man,'" *Houston Post,* January 26, 1952.
15. "12th Man Statue Unveiling Set," *Texas Aggie,* February 1980, 20; "12 Man Statue," *Texas Aggie,* May 1980, 2.
16. Caleb Pirtle, *No Experience Required* (Lindale: Dockery House, 2008), 48–54.
17. Jerry Cooper, "Sherrill Breathes New Life into Twelfth Man Tradition," *Texas Aggie,* March 1983, 26; "Putting a Legend in Uniform," *Texas Aggie,* September 1983, 5.
18. Interview with Bill Youngkin '69, October 23, 2019; "Texas A&M Seeks Restraining Order over '12th Man,'" *USA Today,* January 30, 2006. The license agreement with Seattle was signed on July 21, 2006, following an initial lump sum payment of $100,000 and an annual $5,000 fee.

Chapter 5. Postscript

1. President R. Ames Montgomery, "Presidents Statement to the Board of Trustees," Centre College, January 17, 1924, Centre College Archives; Robertson, *Wonder Team,* 522–527; Charles W. Akers and John W. Carter, *Bo McMillin: Man and Legend* (Louisville: Sulgrave Press, 1989), 73–74. See also "'Miracle Man' of Football Has Been Found and His Name Is Moran," n.p., n.d., Moran Clippings File, Centre College Archives.
2. "McMillin's Brilliant Sprint Gives Centre Victory over Harvard," *St. Louis Post-Dispatch,* October 23, 1921, https://bleacherreport.com/articles/905273; "Charles B. Moran Retired Umpire, 70," *New York Times,* June 15, 1949.
3. Adams, *We Are The Aggies,* 77–78; Kern Tips, *Football—Texas Style* (Garden City, NY: Doubleday, 1964); "Charles B. Moran Retired Umpire, 70," *New York Times,* June 15, 1949. Note: Moran died of heart disease on June 14,

1949, in Horse Cave, Kentucky; *New York Times,* June 15, 1949; Caesar Hohn, *Dutchman on the Brazos: Reminiscences of Caesar "Dutch" Hohn* (Austin: University of Texas Press, 1963), 171. Moran is not listed in Cohane's *Great College Football Coaches of the Twenties and Thirties* (1973) while Bible, Bell, and Norton are all mentioned; yet on page 309 of the book Moran is described as the number-one winningest coach of the era.

4. "State Will Unveil Historical Marker to 'Uncle Charlie' Here," n.p., October 6, 1968, Moran Clippings File, Centre College Archives. A Kentucky historical marker was placed at Farris Stadium, Danville, in 1968. Also the main highway in his home town of Horse Cave was named in Uncle Charlie's honor. The marker on the Centre campus reads as follows:

   "Uncle" Charlie Moran

   Colorful college football coach and Natl. Baseball League umpire. Coached Praying Colonels of Centre College into national football spotlight, 1916–23. First coached, 1898–99, at Bethel College Russellville, Ky. Then held four other coaching positions before going to Texas A. and M., where he coached 1908–13, and at Carlisle Indian School, 1914–15. After seven years at Centre, then Bucknell Univ. 1923–25; Catawba College, 1929–39.

   National League umpire, 1917–39. Officiated at four baseball World Series—1927, 29, 33, 38.

   Born in Nashville, Tenn., 1879. Univ. of Tenn., 1897. Resident of Horse Cave. Died 1949. Interred in the Horse Cave Cemetery.

   Note: Coach Charlie Moran grandson and name sake, Lt. Charles Barthell Moran, USAF, shot down the first enemy airplane in Korean War on June 27, 1950; he was killed-in-action 40 days later on August 7, 1950, and is buried beside his grandfather in the Horse Cave Cemetery, Ky.

5. Bible's response in letter, Albert C. Dick to Dr. R. Ames Montgomery, president, Centre, February 21, 1924, Centre College Archives.
6. Warfield, *Aggies,* 42–43; Ty Cashion, *Pigskin Pulpit: A Social History of Texas High School Football Coaches* (Austin: TSHA, 1998), 94; Ashburn, "D. X. Bible," *Parade,* January 1955, 8, 18; James W. Pohl, "The Bible Decade and the Origin of National Prominence," *SWHQ,* October 1982, 299–320.
7. Maury Goodman and Leonard Lewin, *My Greatest Day in Football* (New York: A. S. Barnes, 1948), 31–35; see also Cohane, *Great College Football Coaches,* 25–29, and Wilbur Evans and H. B. McElroy, *Twelfth Man,* 103–7. Bible's final overall record was 209–64–19. Also in this 1948 publication there is no mention by Bible of King Gill nor is he listed as an A&M team substitute.
8. Dana Bible, audio file, 060980, Cushing Archives; Tips, *Football—Texas Style,* 216. See also "Dana's Decade," *Texas Week,* November 30, 1946, 18–19.

9. "Matty Bell," *Galveston Daily News,* December 3, 1933; Cohane, *Great College Football Coaches,* 16–20; Robertson, *Wonder Team,* 13–15; Evans and McElroy, *Twelfth Man,* 114–17; Goodman and Lewin, *My Greatest Day in Football,* 25–29. Bell selected his greatest day in football as November 30, 1935, when SMU defeated TCU to clinch both the SWC and national crown.
10. Akers and Carter, *Bo McMillin,* 68–69; Watterson, *College Football,* 147–57; Bob Cooper et al., *Total Football: The Official Encyclopedia of the NFL* (New York: Harper Collins, 1997), 986. Watterson does not mention either the Dixie Classic or D. X. Bible in his extensive history of football.
11. Bo McMillin, "M'Millin Tells Why He Coaches Centenary Team," *Alton* (IL) *Evening Telegraph,* November 16, 1922; "'Bo' Buys a Car after Big Season," *Washington Herald,* January 22, 1922; Akers and Carter, *Bo McMillin,* 67–71; Cohane, *Great College Football Coaches,* 158.
12. Akers and Carter, *Bo McMillin,* 73–74, 104–33; Montgomery, "President's Statement to the Board of Trustees," February 5, 1924, Centre College Archives; Watterson, *College Football,* 148–49, 155–57; *New York Times,* April 26, 1926; T. G. Webb, *Battle of the Brazos* (College Station: Texas A&M University Press, 2018), 1–11; "Bo McMillin Nurtured Golden Era," *Paducah Sun-Democrat,* October 24, 1971; "'Bo' McMillin, Grid Coach, Dies at Home," *Columbus Dispatch,* March 31, 1952; "Bo and the Prayin' Colonels," *Sports Illustrated,* November 1968.
13. James R. Woodall, *12 Texas Aggie War Heroes: From World War I to Vietnam* (College Station: Texas A&M University Press, 2016), 218. "Pfaff" is Albert G. Pfaff '25.
14. "Cadet Team Votes New Orleans," *Texas Aggie,* December 6, 1939; "70,000 Sugar Bowl Fans See Aggies Become Nation's No. 1 Team," *Texas Aggie,* January 15, 1940.
15. Interview with Joe Utay, May 21, 1976; Cohane, *Great College Football Coaches,* 155–59; Minutes of the Texas A&M Board of Directors, January 1940; *Longhorn,* 1940, n.p. (Sugar Bowl section); Tips, *Football—Texas Style,* 234–38; Evans and McElroy, *Twelfth Man,* 124–32, 176. See also Mickey Herskowitz, *The 1939 Texas Aggies,* and Donaldson, *Kyle Tough,* 231–42.
16. *Longhorn,* 1922, 376, 396, 400; Chelette, *Class of 1922* (N.p.: n.p., 1985), 71–79; Evans and McElroy, *Twelfth Man,* 89, 107; Adams, *Keepers of the Spirit,* 115–16.
17. Tips, *Football—Texas Style,* 21, 26, 230.
18. "Wilson Departs Sam Houston: Tributes from Bible and Quigley," *Houston Post,* January 20, 1952; interview with Louis Newman, November 14, 2019.
19. *Longhorn,* 1922, 397; "Mac's Facts," *Lubbock Morning Avalanche,* April 30, 1958.

20. Tips, *Football—Texas Style,* 210.
21. Letter, Joe Utay to John Adams, June 1, 1976; contract between Texas A&M and Centre College, "Game of Football and Preliminary Arrangement," Dallas, Texas, December 10, 1921, Utay Papers, Cushing Archives; Ish Haley, "Beyond Joe Utay's Wildest Dreams," 1976 College Bowl Program, Dallas, 1976, 73–74; Lee Cruse, *The Cotton Bowl* (Dallas: Debka, 1964), 1–8. Cruse incorrectly reports that Texas A&M and Centre each received $5,000 for playing in the Dixie Classic.
22. Interview with Utay, May 21, 1976.
23. *Bryan-College Station Eagle,* "Today in Aggie History: September 23, 2020," available at https://myaggienation.com/am_news/today_in_aggie_history/today-in-aggie-history-texas-a-m-plays-the-first-game-at-kyle-field/article_87bd5f4c-4336-11e4-97a7-47a8de2dceb6.html.
24. Interview with Utay, May 21, 1976; White House, purser's book of guest and schedule, May 15, 1937, Franklin D. Roosevelt Library, Hyde Park, New York. The dinner went from 7:45 to 11:55 in the White House executive dining room, with the president retiring at midnight.
25. *Longhorn,* 1909, 196; Adams, *Softly Call the Muster,* 17–22; Adams, *Keepers of the Spirit,* 136–45. George Moore '08 was an assistant coach of the 1909 team.
26. *Longhorn,* 1922, 357, 429.

Bibliography

Primary Sources

Centre College Archives, Danville, Kentucky

Photo digital file: Moran and McMillin

Football Correspondence, 1880–1924

Board of Trustees Minutes, 1917–24

Praying Colonels and Charles B. Moran Clippings File

Cotton Bowl Classic, Arlington, Texas

1976 Cotton Bowl Program, Dallas

Cotton Bowl Media Guide, December 29, 2018

Texas A&M Association of Former Students

The Alumni Quarterly, 1915–20

Texas Aggie, 1921–24

E. King Gill '23 Campus 1964 Muster Speech, introduction by General James Earl Rudder, at www.aggienetwork.com/news/152458/12th-man-story

Association of Former Students, *Directory of Former Students,* 1876–1949

Texas A&M University: Cushing Archives

Dana X. Bible, Audio file, 060980, preservation of 12th Man tradition, interview by M. Tom Harrington '22, October 9, 1969

Longhorn, 1907–48

Aggieland, 1949–2000

Texas A. M. C. Songs and Yells (College Station: YMCA, 1905, 1906, 1907)

The Reveille, 1918–19

Annual Catalogue, Texas A&M, 1890–1930

Dana X. Bible Bio File

Caesar "Dutch" Hohn Papers

Joe Utay '08 Papers

Charlie B. Moran Papers

E. King Gill '24 Papers

Texas A&M Football Papers, 1892–1925

Texas A. & M. College versus Centre College, program, January 2, 1922.

Texas A&M Football Papers

Shrapnel 1, no. 1 (January 1915)

Edward B. Cushing Scrapbook, 1919–23

David J. Finn Scrapbook, 1917–21
Austin E. Burgess Scrapbook, 1911–15
Minutes of the Texas A&M Athletic Council, 1908–41
Minutes of the Association of Former Students, 1900–25
Minutes of the Texas A&M Board of Directors, 1908–41
Bryan Fair Grounds, compiled by Bill Page '76, August 20, 2018.
Football Training Camps, 1910–14, compiled by Bill Page '76, April 8, 2018

Secondary Sources

Books

Adams, John A. *The Fightin' Texas Aggie Defenders of Bataan and Corregidor.* College Station: Texas A&M University Press, 2016.

Adams, John A. *Keepers of the Spirit: The Corps of Cadets at Texas A&M University, 1876–2001.* College Station: Texas A&M University Press, 2001.

Adams, John A. *Over There in the Air: The Fightin Texas Aggies in World War I, 1917–1918.* College Station: Texas A&M University Press, 2019.

Adams, John A. *Softly Call The Muster: The Evolution of a Texas Aggie Tradition.* College Station: Texas A&M University Press, 1979.

Adams, John A. *We Are the Aggies.* College Station: Texas A&M University Press, 1979.

Akers, Charles W., and John W. Carter. *Bo McMillin: Man and Legend.* Louisville: Sulgrave Press, 1989.

Barth, Clarence G. *History of the Twentieth Aero Squadron.* Nashville: Battery Press, 1990.

Benner, Judith A. *Sul Ross: Soldier, Statesman, Educator.* College Station: Texas A&M University Press, 1983.

Bernstein, Patricia. *Ten Dollars to Hate: The Texas Man Who Fought the Klan.* College Station: Texas A&M University Press, 2017.

Bible, Carolyn. *Traditions and Spirit.* Austin: Rolling Green Enterprises, 1990.

Bible, Dana X. *Championship Football: A Guide for Player, Coach and Fan.* New York: Prentice-Hall, 1947.

Blair, Sam. *Aggie Handbook: Stories, Stats and Stuff about Texas A&M Football.* College Station: Mennonite Press, 1996.

Blount, R. E. *Mamas, Don't Let Your Babies Grow Up to Play Football.* Austin: Eakin Press, 1985.

Camp, Walter, ed. *Spalding's Official Foot Ball Guide.* New York: American Sports Publishing, 1915, 1922.

Campbell, Dave. *Dave Campbell's Favorite Texas College Football Stories.* College Station: Texas A&M University Press, 2019.

Carter, Bo, and Mike McKenzie. *Tales from Aggieland.* N.p.: Sports Publishing, 2002.

Casey, Paul D. *The History of Texas A&M College Trouble.* Waco: J. S. Hill, 1908.

Cashion, Ty. *Pigskin Pulpit: A Social History of Texas High School Football Coaches.* Austin: Texas State Historical Association, 1998.

Chelette, Vickie G. *Class of 1922.* N.p.: n.p., 1985.

Cofer, David B. *Early History of Texas A. and M. College through Letters and Papers.* College Station: Association of Former Students, 1952.

Cofer, David B. *Fragments of Early History of Texas A. and M. College.* College Station: Association of Former Students, 1953.

Cohane, Tim. *Great College Football Coaches of the Twenties and Thirties.* New Rochelle: Arlington House, 1973.

The Contribution of Edwin Jackson Kyle to the Development of the Athletic Program of the Agricultural and Mechanical College of Texas. Houston: Adco Press, 1952.

Cooper, Bob, et al. *Total Football: The Official Encyclopedia of the NFL.* New York: Harper Collins, 1997.

Cooper, Jerry C. *Here: The Muster Speeches at Texas A&M University.* College Station: Texas A&M University Press, 2018.

Cruse, Lee. *The Cotton Bowl: A Complete Narrative and Pictorial History.* Dallas: Debka, 1964.

Danzig, Allison. *The History of American Football: Its Great Teams, Players and Coaches.* Englewood Cliffs: Prentice-Hall, 1956.

Danzig, Allison, and Peter Brandwein, eds. *Sport's Golden Age: A Close-Up of the Fabulous Twenties.* New York: Harper and Row, 1948.

Dent, Jim. *The Junction Boys.* New York: St. Martin's Press, 1999.

Dethloff, Henry C. *A Centennial History of Texas A&M University 1876–1976.* 2 vols. College Station: Texas A&M University Press, 1975.

Donaldson, Barbara. *Kyle Tough: The Saga of Texas A&M's Rise to Power in Athletics and Agriculture.* Bryan: Oak Press, 2003.

Evans, Wilbur, and H. B. McElroy. *The Twelfth Man.* Huntsville, AL: Strode, 1974.

Forsyth, John A. *The Aggies and the Horns: 86 Years of Bad Blood and Good Football.* Austin: Texas Monthly Press, 1981.

Goodman, Murray, and Leonard Lewin. *My Greatest Day in Football.* New York: A. S. Barnes, 1948

Herskowitz, Mickey. *The 1939 Texas Aggies: The Greatest Generation's Greatest Team.* Houston: Halcyon Press, 2006.

Hohn, Dutch. *Dutchman on the Brazos.* Austin: University of Texas Press, 1963.

Kleber, John E. *The Kentucky Encyclopedia.* 339–341.

Leftwich, Bill J. *The Corps at Aggieland.* Lubbock: Smoke Signal, 1976.

Loupot, J. E. *Aggie Facts and Figures.* College Station: n.p., 1989. Originally published 1940.

McMurray, Bill. *Texas High School Football.* South Bend: Icarus Press, 1985.
Miller, John J. *The Big Scrum: How Teddy Roosevelt Saved Football.* New York: Harper, 2011.
Minutaglio, Bill. *A Single Star and Bloody Knuckles: A History of Politics and Race in Texas.* Austin: University of Texas Press, 2021.
Nelson, David M. *The Anatomy of a Game: Football, the Rules, and Men Who Made the Game.* Newark: University of Delaware Press, 1994.
Nevels, Cynthia. *Lynching to Belong: Claiming Whiteness through Racial Violence.* College Station: Texas A&M University Press, 2007.
Ousley, Clarence. *History of the Agricultural and Mechanical College of Texas.* College Station: A&M Press, 1935.
Perry, George S. *The Story of Texas A and M.* New York: McGraw Hill, 1951.
Pirtle, Caleb. *No Experience Required: Jackie Sherrell and Texas A&M's 12th Man Kickoff Team.* Dallas: Dockery House, 2007.
Ratliff, Harold V. *Autumn's Mightiest Legions: History of Texas Schoolboy Football.* Waco: Texian Press, 1963.
Ratliff, Harold V. *"I Shook the Hand . . ."* San Antonio: Naylor, 1948.
Revine, Dave. *The Opening Kickoff: The Tumultuous Birth of a Football Nation.* Guilford: Lyons Press, 2014.
Robertson, Robert W. *The Wonder Team: The Story of the Centre College Praying Colonels.* Louisville: Butler Books, 2008.
Rollins, Joseph G. *"Aggies! Y'all Caught That Dam' Ol' Rat Yet?"* San Antonio: Naylor, 1970.
Schoor, Gene. *The Fightin' Texas Aggies: 100 Years of A&M Football.* Dallas: Taylor, 1994.
Stratton, W. K. *Backyard Brawl: Inside the Blood Feud between Texas and Texas A&M.* New York: Three Rivers Press, 2002.
Tips, Kern. *Football—Texas Style.* Garden City, NY: Doubleday, 1964.
Trelease, Allen W. *White Terror: The Ku Klux Klan Conspiracy and Southern Reconstruction.* Westport, CT: Praeger, 1979.
Warfield, Art. *Aggies: A Century of Football Tradition.* New York: Professional Sports Publications, 1994.
Warner, Glenn S. *Football for Coaches and Players.* 1927. Reprint, Carlisle, PA: Tuxedo Press, 2007.
Watterson, John S. *College Football.* Baltimore: John Hopkins University Press, 2000.
Webb, T. G. *Battle of the Brazos: A Texas Football Rivalry, a Riot, and a Murder.* College Station: Texas A&M University Press, 2018.
Whitten, Wiley. *Champions of Naught Six: The Story of the 1906 Cleburne Railroaders.* Fort Worth: Major League Press, 2010.

Articles

Ashburn, Ike. "D. X. Bible." *Texas Parade,* January 1955, 8.

Barnes, Fred. "Unnecessary Roughness." *Wall Street Journal,* September 10, 2011.

"Bo and the Prayin' Colonels." *Sports Illustrated,* November 1968.

Colye, C. J. "The Story of Texas A. and M." *The Texas Magazine,* September 1912.

"Dana's Decade." *Texas Week,* November 30, 1946, 18–19.

"The Dixie Classic." *The Collegiate World,* January 1922, 2, 31.

Doyle, Andrew. "Defeated by the Accreditors: The Rise and Fall of Big-Time Football at Centre College, 1915–1926." *The Register of the Kentucky Historical Society,* Autumn 2017, 471–524.

Haley, Ish. "Beyond Joe Utay's Wildest Dreams." 1976 Cotton Bowl Program, Dallas, 1976, 73–74.

"Moran, Centre Coach, Former Nashville Star." *New Scimitar,* November 29, 1919.

Nicar, Jim. "The Rose Bowl That Was Almost in Austin." *The Alcalde,* March 2006, 110–11.

Pohl, James W. "The Bible Decade and the Origin of National Prominence." *SWHQ,* October 1982, 299–320.

"The Praying Football Team." *Literary Digest,* December 11, 1920, 39.

Smylie, Vernon. "A&M's First 'Twelfth Man' Tells How Tradition Was Born." *Houston Press,* January 19, 1956.

"Texas A&M Celebrates Black History and Achievement," *Texas A&M Today,* January 31, 2020.

"Texas A&M to Commemorate 50th Anniversary of Admission of Woman, Minority Inclusiveness," *Texas A&M Today,* August 27, 2013.

Utay, Joe. "Southwestern Conference Foot Ball." *Spalding's Intercollegiate Official Foot Ball Guide,* ed. Walter Camp, 75–77. N.p.: Spalding, 1922.

Watts, Arthur P. "The Romantic Days of the Flying Wedge." *Dallas Morning News,* November 17, 1929.

Dissertations, Manuscripts, and Presentations

DeBella, Joseph A. C. "The History of Physical Education at TAMU, 1876–1988." Dissertation, Texas A&M University, December 1989.

Dunn, Jeff. "A History of the Texas A&M Football Fight Songs: 1902–1950." 40th Reunion, Class of '76, College Station, October 21, 2016.

Interviews

E. King Gill '24, misc.

Joe Utay '08, May 21, 1976

Gary Utay '69, May 1, 2016

James V. "Pinky" Wilson, March 19, 1975, and June 14, 1976

Sam Houston Sanders, July 21, 1982, by Charles Crawford, University of Tennessee Archives, Memphis, TN

Robert Robertson, September 6, 2019
Jeff Dunn '76, September 8, 2019
Asa Hunt, May 25, 1975
E. E. McQuillen '20, June 2, 1975
Ray Bowen '58, October 12, 2019
Bill Page '76, October 3 and 10, 2019
Alan Cannon '84, October 16, 2019
Bill Youngkin '69, October 23, 2019
Louis Newman, November 14, 2019
Dave Campbell, October 7, 2019
Robert A. Epstein '44, February 10, 2020

Newspapers

Austin American-Statesman, 1910–24
Boston Daily Post, 1919–22
Bryan Daily Eagle, 1892–1924
Chicago Daily Tribune, 1922
Columbus [OH] *Dispatch*, 1952
Dallas Morning News, 1910–24
Danville [KY] *Advocate-Messenger*, 1921–24
Des Moines Capital, 1922
El Paso Herald, 1910–25
Fort Worth Star-Telegram, 1910–25
Galveston Daily News, 1885–1924
Houston Chronicle, 1909
Houston Daily Post, 1900–1924
Houston Press, 1956
Lexington [KY] *Courier-Journal*, 1918–24
Lexington Daily Leader, 1921
Los Angeles Times, 1921–22
Lubbock Morning Avalanche, 1958
New York Sun, 1920–23
New York Times, 1885–1924
Paducah [KY] *Sun-Democrat*, 1971
San Antonio Express-News, 1910–24
South Bend News-Times, 1922
St. Louis Post-Dispatch, 1921
Temple Daily Telegram, 1914
Texas A&M University *Battalion*, 1893–1925, 1938–39, 1941, 1955, 1976, 2019
Waco Daily Times-Herald, 1908
Washington [DC] *Herald*, 1922
Weatherford Daily Herald, 1922

Index

Note: Page numbers in *italics* indicate illustrations.